THE LAYMAN'S BIBLE COMMENTARY

This 25-volume series has been carefully designed to meet the need for a Bible study tool in layman's language. Within its pages the meaning of the Holy Scripture is opened up, passage by passage, in stimulating terms.

All space in the LBC volumes is used for thorough exposition. The editors and authors are outstanding interpreters of the Old and New Testaments, chosen for their ability to write within the layman's grasp. (Note: opposite the title page is a complete listing of volumes and writers.)

In the LBC, technical terms are avoided (including Greek and Hebrew words), and every effort is bent toward making this commentary useful to the greatest number of students and teachers.

Many lay men and women will find the LBC volumes excellent for personal and family study of the Bible. Teachers and other leaders in church schools will use them for lesson preparation and background. Ministers, Bible study groups, libraries, editors, and writers will find this commentary of great value.

The *Layman's Bible Commentary* is published in Canada by The Ryerson Press of Toronto, and throughout the British Commonwealth by SCM Press of London.

THE LAYMAN'S BIBLE COMMENTARY

THE LAYMAN'S BIBLE COMMENTARY
IN TWENTY-FIVE VOLUMES

THE LAYMAN'S
BIBLE COMMENTARY

Balmer H. Kelly, *Editor*

Donald G. Miller   *Associate Editors*   Arnold B. Rhodes

Dwight M. Chalmers, *Editor, John Knox Press*

VOLUME 4

THE BOOK OF
LEVITICUS

THE BOOK OF
NUMBERS

James L. Mays

71–31951

JOHN KNOX PRESS
RICHMOND, VIRGINIA

Published in Great Britain by SCM Press Ltd., London. Published simultaneously in Canada by The Ryerson Press, Toronto.

Third printing 1971

International Standard Book Number: 0-8042-3022-6

Library of Congress Catalog Card Number: 59-10454

Printed in the United States of America

PREFACE

The LAYMAN'S BIBLE COMMENTARY is based on the conviction that the Bible has the Word of good news for the whole world. The Bible is not the property of a special group. It is not even the property and concern of the Church alone. It is given to the Church for its own life but also to bring God's offer of life to all mankind —wherever there are ears to hear and hearts to respond.

It is this point of view which binds the separate parts of the LAYMAN'S BIBLE COMMENTARY into a unity. There are many volumes and many writers, coming from varied backgrounds, as is the case with the Bible itself. But also as with the Bible there is a unity of purpose and of faith. The purpose is to clarify the situations and language of the Bible that it may be more and more fully understood. The faith is that in the Bible there is essentially one Word, one message of salvation, one gospel.

The LAYMAN'S BIBLE COMMENTARY is designed to be a concise non-technical guide for the layman in personal study of his own Bible. Therefore, no biblical text is printed along with the comment upon it. This commentary will have done its work precisely to the degree in which it moves its readers to take up the Bible for themselves.

The writers have used the Revised Standard Version of the Bible as their basic text. Occasionally they have differed from this translation. Where this is the case they have given their reasons. In the main, no attempt has been made either to justify the wording of the Revised Standard Version or to compare it with other translations.

The objective in this commentary is to provide the most helpful explanation of fundamental matters in simple, up-to-date terms. Exhaustive treatment of subjects has not been undertaken.

In our age knowledge of the Bible is perilously low. At the same time there are signs that many people are longing for help in getting such knowledge. Knowledge of and about the Bible is, of course, not enough. The grace of God and the work of the Holy Spirit are essential to the renewal of life through the Scriptures. It is in the happy confidence that the great hunger for the Word is a sign of God's grace already operating within men, and that the Spirit works most wonderfully where the Word is familiarly known, that this commentary has been written and published.

THE EDITORS AND
THE PUBLISHERS

THE BOOKS OF
LEVITICUS AND NUMBERS

INTRODUCTION

For most of us today the Books of Leviticus and Numbers are territory as barren and unknown as the dry, trackless wilderness in which much of their story is set. In Bible study one tends to take a giant stride from the exciting making of the Covenant at Sinai (Exod. 19-24) to the plains of Moab to hear the great moving sermons of Moses to the People of God, delivered just before his death (Deuteronomy). The mass of material in Exodus 25-40, Leviticus, and Numbers is ignored or skimmed over lightly. After all, why should twentieth-century Christians bother? Exodus 25-40 is mostly about planning and building the Tabernacle. Since we do not use tabernacles any more, its expansive, repetitious description hardly encourages us to study. The best we can do here is turn the material over to the children as a project in vacation Bible school—they might enjoy making a papier-mâché tabernacle. And Leviticus? Judging from its name, it must be about the Levites, that long-since extinct tribe of clerics who looked after the Tabernacle and Temple. Numbers would deal with the process of dividing the Israelites up into tribes and categories and of counting how many there were in each division.

There is some justification for these impressions, but not much. Actually, the names of the books are creations of convenience. They arose when the Hebrew Pentateuch was translated into Greek and names were invented for each of the divisions (five, because the material was traditionally written on five scrolls). The Jews named each of these divisions by a phrase from its opening sentence. To Leviticus they gave the title "And he called" (see Lev. 1:1); Numbers was appropriately named "In the wilderness" (Num. 1:1). The Greek translators, because the former deals extensively with the priesthood, which was often called "levitical," chose the name Leviticus, although there is more about the Levites in Numbers. The second book they called

"Numbers" because in it the People of God are numbered. It does have two accounts of a census made of the Israelites (Num. 1 and 26), but these two chapters are far from defining its content.

The fundamental fact to be faced when one opens his Bible to Leviticus and Numbers for study is that these two are an inseparable part of a larger whole. They are not independent books which carry their meaning on their own, and they will not be understood unless studied in their literary and narrative context. They are the middle part of a continuous story which runs from Genesis through Deuteronomy and, indeed, on into Joshua. The whole narrative is the introduction to the Bible and tells why and how there came to be a People of God living in Palestine. It begins at the Creation and reaches its climax with the conquest of the Promised Land. So the reader must think constantly about what has gone before and what comes after, as he studies Leviticus and Numbers. Their concerns and characters and movement are of a piece with the other four books.

This means also that Leviticus and Numbers play a crucial part in an understanding of the others. One does not leave Sinai and arrive in the Promised Land without first finishing the encampment at the Mount of God and then enduring with Israel the long, arduous, and painful way through the wilderness. For the story itself is the way Israel testifies to and learns the true knowledge of God. It is, as will be explained below, Israel's confession of faith. To drop out the middle part would be as disastrous as omitting the second division of the Apostles' Creed.

It is indispensable, then, to get the context of Leviticus and Numbers clear. This can be done from three angles or points of view: First, the way Leviticus-Numbers fits into the present form of the first six books of the Bible; second, the part of Israel's history about which they tell; third, the literary history which they share with the others.

The Context and Content

The first six books of the Old Testament tell a story which runs from the creation of the world (Gen. 1-2) to a ceremony to renew the Covenant between the Lord and Israel in the Promised Land (Joshua 24). There is a great deal more in these six books than the narrative itself, but it is the narrative which gives the whole its essential unity and furnishes the framework in which all the other material appears. This story is the introduction to the faith and life of the People of God, the indispensable historical and theological background to what Israel believes and does in her existence before God. When the people of Israel speak of the Lord they mean the God who created the world and man, who called the fathers and set their present under the future of the promise, who revealed his name to Moses and saved the Israelites when they were in bondage in Egypt, who made covenant with them at Sinai, who brought them through the wilderness and gave them the land in which they live. It is first of all in this *holy history,* a history brought about and interpreted by God, that Israel has her knowledge of God. His name is "the LORD," and the name points to the Being who has become manifest in the story. Or, when Israel thinks about its own identity, it thinks of itself as a work of the Lord, created and formed in the process of the holy history. Israel is the People of God because he chose them in the fathers, made them his people through the Covenant, preserved and defended and chastised them in the wilderness, and brought them into the Promised Land. They owe their existence to the election of the Lord. Their life is to be lived according to his will as made known in the Covenant requirements. Or, when Israel asks why God has chosen their nation, they remember that the holy history, which begins with the Creation, is followed by the account of man's sin. God is the Lord, but man is in rebellion. Israel is a part of the humanity which seeks by itself to decide what is good, and usurps the lordship of God in his world. The election of Israel is God's way of bringing some back to trust and obedience. As the Covenant People they are the first step in God's strategy to reclaim his world by grace instead of judgment. God's lordship over them is a sign that one day all the kingdoms of this world shall become the Kingdom of the Lord. Israel's very existence is prophetic of what is to be for all creation.

Leviticus and Numbers are part of this theological history by which the knowledge of God is declared and preserved in the Old Testament Church. The way they fit into the whole may be seen through an interpretative outline such as the following:

Genesis 1-11. God creates the world and man, and man rebels against God's lordship.

Genesis 12-50. God chooses the fathers to live under his promise to bless them and, through them, the whole earth.

Exodus 1-18. God reveals his name ("the LORD") and manifests his lordship over nature and history by the deliverance
of Israel from Egypt.

Exodus 19—Numbers 10. God sets up his Covenant with Israel, giving them his instructions by which to live, instituting
the worship of himself as the center of their life, and ordering and arranging their existence around the paramount fact
of his presence in their midst.

Numbers 11—Deuteronomy 34. God brings his people through
the wilderness, teaching them by his help and his wrath what
it means to exist in history under his lordship, and leads them
to the edge of the Promised Land, where they are prepared
for life in it.

Joshua 1-24. God gives Israel the Promised Land and renews
the Covenant with them, to establish their existence there
under his lordship.

One can see from this outline that the principal subject of these
six books is the story of Israel before it appears as a nation in
Palestine. The concentration is on the sequence from the Exodus
to the entry into the Promised Land, telling us how Israel came
to be living in Palestine as the Covenant People of the Lord. To
this main story Genesis is a twofold introduction. The second
part, about the fathers, tells how and why Israel is the nation
which becomes the Covenant People in Palestine. The first part
sets the whole in connection with creation and within all mankind, to show that Israel's history is God's response to the problem of world history and human tragedy. Moreover, the outline
shows how Leviticus opens in the midst of the principal story.
All of Leviticus and the first ten chapters of Numbers are part of
the story of the institution of the Covenant. The remainder of
Numbers is the first part of the section on Israel's preparation, in
the wilderness and the plains of Moab, to enter the Promised
Land, a section completed in the sermons of Moses before he
dies (the Book of Deuteronomy).

With this larger framework in mind we can move in closer to
see just what Leviticus and Numbers contribute to the total movement.

Leviticus 1—Numbers 10:28. These chapters open in the midst
of the second part of the Sinai story. In the first part, Exodus
19-24, the Covenant proper is concluded and God's instruction
for the fundamental life of Israel is given in the Decalogue and

the Covenant Law. In Exodus 25 the second part begins with God's instruction about the Tabernacle. The Tabernacle sequence reaches its climax in Exodus 40:34-38 when "the glory of the LORD" descends from Mount Sinai's summit to rest in and fill the Tabernacle. This dramatic and mysterious event is the basic clue to what the entire second part of the Sinai section is about. The fundamental reality of the Covenant is the relationship of God and Israel: "I will be your God and you will be my people." By the Covenant, God said to Israel, "Lo, I am with you." The Tabernacle is the provision for God's presence; it is his place in the midst of Israel; by it God shows himself to be the center of Israel's life. Leviticus and Numbers 1:1—10:28 are a continuation of the Tabernacle sequence, for the defining concern in all their variety is the arrangement of Israel's life around the Presence at the center. *God is holy*. This affirmation is the presupposition of the entire second section of the Sinai story. The affirmation raises a question. How do profane and sinful men arrange their entire existence around the wondrous Holy One who comes to be in their midst? Leviticus 1:1—Numbers 10:28 moves from one area to another of Israel's life, dealing with the new situation created when the Holy appears in the midst of common life. How shall men offer themselves in adoration, gratitude, and confession to the Holy God? The manual of sacrifice (Lev. 1-7) is the answer. How shall profane man reach to the Holy and the Holy to sinners in the commerce of worship? The consecrated mediatorial priesthood (Lev. 8-10) is the answer. How shall the holiness of God dominate and sanctify profane life? The manual for purification (Lev. 11-16) is the answer. How shall the people obey the holiness of God so that the "holy" becomes a way of life? The law of holiness (Lev. 17-27) is the answer. How shall the nation be organized and arranged in its public existence so that its way through history is a pilgrimage guided by the Holy? The preparation to leave Sinai to move toward the fulfillment of God's promise (Num. 1-10) is the answer. Exodus 25—Numbers 10, then, is the completion of the Covenant arrangement. Exodus 25-40 describes the great fact of Israel's Covenant existence—the Holy in their midst. Leviticus 1:1—Numbers 10:28 shows what the Presence means for Israel's life.

Numbers 11-36. These chapters belong to the section in which Israel leaves Sinai, moves through the wilderness, finally camps in the plains of Moab, and there prepares to enter the Promised

Land. Chapters 11-21 follow Israel from Sinai to the plains of Moab, and tell of happenings along the way, happenings between God and Israel by which the way of God with his people becomes clearer. The story moves from camp to camp as Israel progresses toward her goal, but the concern is with far more than the mere geography of Israel's route. How does a sinful people exist and move through the wilderness of this world under the lordship of God? What is the nature of the way from election to consummation? How does the Lord maintain his people on the way? It is these kinds of questions which chapters 11-21 of Numbers raise and speak about. What happened to Israel on the way through the wilderness has meaning for the Chosen People on their way under God in all times. In the rest of Numbers, chapters 22-36, Israel is in camp in the plains of Moab preparing to cross the Jordan into the Land of Promise. All the varied material in these chapters is held together by that basic motif of preparation. During the rigorous and tragic years in the wilderness, one generation has passed away. Now the second generation must be confirmed in the Covenant order. The Balaam story (chs. 22-24) puts the promise to Abraham once more over the people. The first encounter with the gods of the land is undergone (ch. 25). The people are numbered once more (ch. 26), and instructions for their life in the land across the Jordan are given (chs. 27-36). Moses is readied for his death, and arrangement is made for Joshua's assumption of leadership. After these chapters, Deuteronomy comes with its rolling sermons by Moses, putting afresh the Covenant truth and the Covenant life. The whole is meant to be a witness to Israel in all times that only those who live as the Covenant People can experience the blessings of God's promise.

This, then, is the way in which Leviticus and Numbers fit into the larger whole of Genesis—Joshua. Their location is part of their meaning. The interpreter must keep this total context in mind as he begins with Leviticus and reads each of the sections in it and Numbers.

The Historical Period

Leviticus and Numbers cover a very short segment of the Old Testament story of Israel. The entire story from Abraham to the time of the Book of Daniel occupies most of two thousand years. The narrative in the two books of Leviticus and Numbers involves hardly more than the life span of one generation. The "forty years in the wilderness" is an almost stereotyped phrase in the Old Testament; it is approximately the period about which Leviticus and Numbers tell. The Exodus from Egypt occurred during the reign of Pharaoh Rameses II early in the thirteenth century. During the second half of that century Israel moved into Palestine under Joshua. Thus, the historical period of these books runs approximately from 1280 to 1240 B.C.

Leviticus opens with Israel camped at the foot of Mount Sinai. The traditional identification of Sinai with Jebel Musa, a high peak in the southern part of the Sinai peninsula, is probably correct. Some scholars have sought a location for Sinai further to the north and east of the Gulf of Aqabah, the home territory of Midian. Though there is no certainty in the matter, the site in the southern part of the peninsula of Sinai fits the qualifications of biblical tradition best.

On leaving Sinai the Israelites followed a route northward toward the boundary of Canaan, apparently intending to enter the land from the south. The camps along the way which are mentioned in Numbers can no longer be located precisely. Nor is this surprising. The camp sites of nomads, even if they were customary ones used repeatedly, leave little in the way of remains as a clue to archaeologists of the present. However, the location of Kadesh, where Israel set up a base camp for the assault on Canaan, is well established at a spring-watered oasis, some fifty miles south of Beer-sheba.

In the mid-thirteenth century, Canaan was already occupied by a variety of peoples whose names are given in various lists in the Bible (for example, Num. 13:29). The principal groups were the Canaanites along the coastal plain and in the more fertile valleys. In the hill country the Amorites were settled. They shared that territory with such peoples as the Jebusites, Hittites, Hivites, and the like. The Israelites were demoralized by the dimension of the opposition facing them, failed to mount the assault as an enterprise of holy war under God, and were grievously defeated at Hormah (Num. 13:1—14:45). The tribes fell back to Kadesh and remained there for a generation.

When the Israelites moved out once again in their trek to Canaan, they headed east to circle the Dead Sea in order to approach the land by way of the Jordan Valley. The itinerary in Numbers 33 gives the route and its encampments in meticulous detail, but once again most of the places can no longer be identified. The general course of the route, however, is clear. The newly formed kingdoms of Edom and Moab stood across the best way to Israel's goal, the ancient caravan route called "the King's Highway." Avoiding a clash with these people, the Israelites went up the valley of the Arabah and turned east at the lower end of the Dead Sea to follow the border between Moab and Edom along the Brook Zered. They then circled to the east around Moab until the River Arnon was crossed.

At that juncture Israel had no choice but to enter the territory of the Amorite kingdoms dominating the eastern side of the Jordan River. A successful war with Sihon was followed by a victory over the kingdom of Og. With the Transjordan territory north of Moab in their control, the Israelites made another long encampment in the plains of Moab at the lower end of the Jordan River. At this point the Book of Numbers comes to an end. The story of the move into Canaan is taken up in Joshua.

The importance of these years in the wilderness for the formation of Israel as the Covenant People of the Lord and their growth in understanding the significance of their new identity can be measured only by a close inspection of the two books of Leviticus and Numbers, especially the middle chapters of Numbers, and by attention to the way in which Israel in later history always looked back to the wilderness. Those years were dominated by the towering figure of Moses. It is from Numbers, as much as from Exodus, that we learn the crucial meaning of his role. Here we come to know the spiritual giant whose authority and meekness, enthusiasm and agony, success and failure, formed the human instrument by which God disclosed himself and his will for the sake of getting himself a People.

The Literary History

Though Leviticus and Numbers have a historical setting in the thirteenth century B.C., they are not to be thought of as history in a technical sense. To compare them and the rest of the books in the Pentateuch to the "histories" which scholars write today is misleading. Our modern critical histories are efforts to understand and reconstruct the past just as it was. They are interested primarily in the facts about the events of some period and seek to be as objective and unbiased as possible in reconstructing what happened. In their concern to deal only with what can, from acceptable evidence, be demonstrated as real, they do not reckon with the Divine, with the presence or absence of God in certain human affairs.

Leviticus and Numbers were not written for such reasons or by such methods. They do deal with what has happened in the past and do tell stories about it, but it is not because they are interested in knowing just what happened. Rather, the Israelite tells what has happened for the sake of knowing God. Remembering what had gone before was a matter of faith; it was a theological enterprise. The God of the Covenant revealed himself to Israel in the course of the migrations of Abraham and Jacob, through the escape from Egyptian bondage, during the encampment and at Sinai, during the wandering in the wilderness, and in the victories won in the conquest of Canaan. It was this revelation that made the past important. Israel told about what had happened in such a way that the stories conveyed knowledge of God. Who is the true God? What is he like? What is he about in the world and its affairs? What is his attitude toward men and how does he deal with them? What does he desire of men? How are men to live before him? Israel's narratives about the past are shaped and dominated by concern with such questions. Because they are, the stories stretch the narrative form so that it can include this drama of God and man within the stream of what happened. The stories take on the quality of vision and poetry, because the dimension of reality with which they deal cannot be captured in the usual terms which describe human experience. Therefore, the truth of these stories does not primarily depend on their correspondence to just what actually happened in visible, external fashion. Truth here lies first of all at the level of the narrative's meaning for the knowledge of God. The question to ask is not the question of modern history: "How can I know this happened?" Instead one is to ask, "What is here offered faith so that I truly know what to believe and to do?" The history in the Pentateuch, then, is of a peculiar kind. It has a transcendent depth which gives it a permanent contemporaneity. It is really about the past—that fact can never be ignored. But it has to do with the present, the time in which it is told, precisely because it conveys the knowledge of the God who is still God.

There is another kind of depth to these books of which the reader today ought to be aware. The basic story of God's way with Israel and its ancestors before the permanent settlement in Canaan is told, not once, but four times. In the present form of the Pentateuch all four versions of the basic story have been used to make up the whole. One version is found in Deuteronomy in the speeches of Moses; it stands clearly separate and is easy to read in its own right. The other three have been woven together so that in most chapters the merged material reads along quite well as one story. At some places the same story is told twice, in a distinctive form for each version. There are two creation stories at the beginning of Genesis (Gen. 1:1—2:4 and 2:5-25) and two stories of Moses' call (Exod. chs. 3-4 and 6: 2-9). In some places the interweaving of the versions is particularly clear (for example, in the narrative of the spies in Numbers 13-14, or the narrative of Baal of Peor in Numbers 25).

It may be helpful to remember that in the New Testament there are four separate accounts of the life of Jesus Christ in the four Gospels. No two of the four are wholly alike; each has its own character and contributes its own approach to understanding the life of our Lord. The Gospel of John is particularly distinctive in comparison with the other three, which are so similar in the material which they contain that they are called "synoptic." Now if Matthew, Mark, and Luke had been merged into one big Gospel using material from each, the result would have been somewhat like the literary situation we have in Genesis through Numbers. In fact, something like this was attempted several times early in the history of the Church before the Canon of Scripture was fixed; but in the end, it was the four separate Gospels which remained the Church's Scripture.

In the long history of Israel under quite different circumstances the merging process did occur; and the combined form won its place as the present Pentateuch.

The earliest literary work telling the theological history of Israel was written during the reign of David and Solomon in Jerusalem. It began at the Creation and possibly ran through the Conquest. Because this work used the proper name of Israel's God from the beginning, it has been called "J," after the German pronunciation of the sacred Tetragrammaton (YHWH in Hebrew; "Yahweh" in English; often in popular pronunciation, "Jehovah"; "LORD" in the Revised Standard Version).

In the north, among the ten tribes that seceded from Judah and her king after Solomon's reign, the second version appeared.

It is represented by the sign "E" because in it the general Hebrew word for "God" (Elohim) is used until after the revelation of God's proper name in Exodus 3. This version displays the interests and outlook of the prophetic circles which were active in the Northern Kingdom. It was probably written down in the late ninth or early eighth century.

When the Assyrians overwhelmed the Northern Kingdom, only Judah was left. Because there was such a firm belief that God had called all twelve tribes to be his people, concern lest the literature of faith belonging to the north be lost led to the joining and interweaving of "E" with "J." As a result there was once again one story of God's way with Israel. The merged literary work is referred to as "JE." The combination is generally so intimate that, although one can detect signs of the two strands, it is impossible to separate them neatly. (In the comment this conflated form of the two earlier stories is simply identified as JE and an attempt at separation is made only where exposition requires it.)

During the reform of religion led by King Josiah late in the seventh century, the basic material of Deuteronomy was discovered. Its account of the Mosaic era is cast in the form of a succinct oration. This Deuteronomic strand ("D") is found from Deuteronomy through the Books of Kings.

The final telling of the pre-Canaan story took place during the exilic period in the sixth century. This time, the work was done by the priests, who had become important in Israel's religion with the end of the monarchy; and it is called "P" after the circles in which it originated. This latest version is characterized by an interest in the institutions and ordinances of Israel's worship, and it served to guide the restoration of Israel's national religious life around the Second Temple in the years when the exiles returned from Babylon. It was sometime during the early postexilic period that JE was incorporated into P, with D included at the end, to create the present Pentateuch.

The greater part of the material in Leviticus and Numbers comes from P, the Priestly source. Leviticus takes up the P sequence which, beginning at Exodus 25, tells about the Tabernacle. The P material runs without interruption through Leviticus and on into Numbers, through Numbers 10:28. From that point on through Numbers 25 the JE source furnishes the basic narrative structure, but with generous help from P. Then, in Numbers 26, P takes over alone and continues to the end of the book.

Obviously, then, we do not have in the two books a "history" in the usual sense of that word—that is, a record of just what happened in the generation of the wilderness in the mid-thirteenth century, a record based exclusively on the evidence of sources and data contemporary with the events. Leviticus and Numbers, along with the rest of the Pentateuch, were not written by Moses or any other Israelite of the thirteenth century. But to view that fact in a negative, disillusioned way would be to miss the real purpose of the Pentateuch, and to misunderstand what it intends to be.

There are a number of things to be kept in mind as we think about the way these books came into existence. First of all, it is clear that the material in them was not invented at the time when it was written down. The best available evidence does indicate that P was put in its final form in the sixth century. But the man who prepared the final draft did not think up its contents imaginatively; he was preserving very ancient lore that went deep into the past behind him, writing it down precisely because this was what the priestly circles remembered from the past. The great theologian who wrote J during the early years of the monarchy was not an author in our sense of the word. He was recording at that point what Israel remembered about God's way with her. Over and over again, where archaeology has turned up the kind of data against which the historical events in his record can be checked, the record has been shown to have a sure footing in the time and the events about which it tells. The books are not history, but they are *historical* in quality. Behind their stories lie real people and actual events from which they derive.

Moreover, the tradition which came down to the writers told about far more than the original event itself. One might say that the historical memory itself lived through the intervening time, participated in its history, and indeed shaped and determined it. What the tribes in Canaan remembered about Moses was preserved because it was the source material of their faith. It was not the property of some bureau of archives and records, jealously guarded in its original form. It was the instrument and weapon of the inspired religious leaders of Israel. It was taught and applied, preached, meditated on, used in liturgy, and sung at worship. Men of faith turned to it to seek its meaning and guidance in their own times. As the material was used, the meaning and relevance found in it were incorporated in the material itself.

What the life and faith of Moses said became under the inspiration of God part of the tradition about Moses. And the earlier form of the material attracted other new stories which unfolded in larger, fuller ways its basic motifs. The tradition, then, not only grew out of history, but had its own living history which contributed to its nature. Thus, what we have in the combined sources is not so much a history of Israel as a story of the Word of God.

Throughout Leviticus and Numbers one encounters material which represents the religious situation in a later time than that of Moses. This is particularly true of the substantial blocks of laws and regulations in both books. Leviticus opens with a large manual to guide the practice of sacrifice (chs. 1-7); in its present form it represents the practice of the priests in the late monarchy and in the Second Temple, after the Exile. There are regulations in Leviticus and Numbers (Lev. 9; Num. 3, 4, 8, 18), dealing with the Aaronic priesthood and the Levitical clergy, which reflect the final stages of the development of priesthood in Israel. This material, as well as most of the rest in P, is introduced by the formula, "And God said to Moses" (or "Moses and Aaron"). The writers did not present the material in this way in order to falsify history, but to interpret it to faith. The material is for them "Mosaic"; it extends, applies, and unfolds the original principles of belief given through Moses. It is the will of the God of Moses who set up the Covenant at Sinai. By putting the material in the pentateuchal story at the point of Sinai, Israel's theologians were saying that it must be understood and held in the context of the original Covenant. Sinai is never just past history; as the Covenant People, Israel is forever assembled before it. And Moses is the constant contemporary of men in the Old Testament Church.

In the two books, then, we do not have a uniform work, such as would be produced by one author, writing at one time. And the history which contributes to their contents is longer than the scenes which they portray. What binds the material together is not a humanly created uniformity, but the unity of faith under the revelation of God. Here speak many times and many voices as a choir of witnesses to the one God.

The Message

Any attempt here to summarize the meaning of Leviticus and

Numbers for the believer today would be a poor anticipation of the commentary that is to follow. One cannot reduce the variety and depth of such comprehensive books to a few ideas or categories and do them justice. But the reader may need some preliminary guidance about the way one apprehends the meaning in these books which is valid for faith today. For no sooner do we open the Book of Leviticus than we are faced with a detailed set of instructions about how the five central types of animal and grain sacrifice are to be offered. Some may find this information quite interesting, and others may be dismayed at the prospect of tracing its tedious detail. But obviously the simple information does not exhaust our concern. The fact is, we do not offer sacrifice in the church any more. Therefore one cannot be satisfied with a simple question about what is said in plain language. The quest of faith after the knowledge of God must penetrate the surface of this material to grasp the relevance that lies at a deeper level.

This is not to say that the believer of today is to be unconcerned with the plain fact of what is said. Brush that aside and we have no way to get at a helpful meaning of use to us in our lives of trust and obedience, for the meaning comes through just those words, or it does not come at all. Moreover, knowing about *what* Israel did is crucial for us today. The history of the Church is an extension of the history of Israel; the past on which these books open a door is our own past. Many things we do and many ideas we use in the Christian Church have their origin and assume their significance in the time and experience of Israel. When we use a central place of worship, work with a ministry, give order to our corporate churchly life, or think of life as sacrificial, then we are invoking realities and conceptions which took their rise in part in these two books. We cannot use these concepts and do these things properly and meaningfully apart from their origin on which they and we depend. The Church and its faith arose in history; therefore, knowledge of our past is really an important kind of self-knowledge. The stories of Moses and of what happened in the wilderness are as important to us as Christians as the stories of the Pilgrims and the Revolutionary War are for us as Americans.

But these books do more than tell us about our past; as part of the Canon, they also claim an authority and capacity to speak to us in the present, to guide and shape our living as people of faith through their "word." To apprehend this relevance, the believer must ask not only about the *what*, but also about the *why* and the *whither* of this material. *What* God said to Israel at various times in her history had direct relevance precisely for that time and for the situation in which Israel found herself. Behind the *what* of these messages, penetrating real history through inspired men, was a *why* and a *whither*. The *why* rests in the nature and will of God, in what he is like and what he wants of men. The *whither* lies in the future purpose of God in his yet unrealized goal for men and their history.

It is this *why* and *whither* within the *what* of the words in Leviticus and Numbers which the believer must seek. Since the time when God spoke to Moses in the wilderness, or when the Aaronic priesthood was established, or when certain ceremonies for cleansing were ordained, time and history have moved on. The biblical revelation takes time seriously and realistically. Within the Old Testament period itself the *what* of certain institutions, laws, and ways of worship changed with developing, shifting circumstances. At the end of the Old Testament stands the Day of the Lord, when God came to man as man in Jesus Christ. The Old Testament is now read in the light of the total history, and especially in the light of its fulfillment in the Lord Jesus. Its *what* belongs to the past, an important, crucial past, but nonetheless the past. We no longer practice the same rituals of purification or have the descendants of Aaron as our priests. But the *why*—what we learn in these books of God's nature and will —and the *whither*—the directional quality of the material as it points toward the consummation to which God is leading mankind—these abide and speak to us today. God's will and goal remain unchanged. He is the same yesterday, today, and forever. Over and over again in the experience of the Church this potential, this capacity of the material to confront the Church as God's Word in the here and now of the present, has been manifested as reality.

In studying Leviticus and Numbers no simple set of rules will suffice to guide one through the variety of material. With different passages we are set down at quite different vantage points as interpreters. In Leviticus 19:18 we read, "You shall love your neighbor as yourself," and we confront words whose plain meaning claims us directly; indeed, this command has been validated and delivered to the Church by Jesus (Mark 12:31). The lovely phrases of the "Aaronic benediction" (Num. 6:22-26) are a treasured part of our liturgical heritage; when we hear them we feel that they are spoken immediately to us. But when one comes to the rules for purifying women after childbirth (Lev. 12), it is necessary to ask about the whole function and meaning behind the notion of being "unclean," why it was important to Israel, how God used it in Israel's life to guide the Covenant People, and what the "future" of the idea is in the New Testament fulfillment. We no longer offer sacrifice as Leviticus 1-7 requires. But Jesus Christ has entered into the sphere of the sacrificial to offer himself as sacrifice on our behalf. His death for our sake drives us back to Leviticus to learn why God adopted and ordered sacrifice for Israel as a way of approach to him. The *why* and the *whither* of the sacrifice on the great Day of Atonement (Lev. 16) become a moving interpretation and dramatic testimony to God's gracious act for sinners. Sacrifice is done away with as a liturgical activity of man; but it is not cancelled out. It is caught up and fulfilled in Calvary's Cross, and persists in the moral and personal will to discipleship.

These, then, are the characteristics of our approach as we seek to study Leviticus and Numbers as part of the Scriptures of the Church. We stand in our own time with its peculiar needs and circumstances, knowing the full story of God's way from Abraham to Jesus Christ, waiting in faith for the final consummation of the New Creation, in which we are to share through the resurrection. So in humble expectation, knowing that often we shall come short of the *why* and *whither,* we open to Leviticus and find, "The LORD called Moses, and spoke to him . . ." The truest equipment of the interpreter is earnest prayer that this very speaking shall also take place for him.

OUTLINE

At Sinai: The Arrangement of Israel's Life Around the Holy. Leviticus 1:1—Numbers 10:28

Introduction (Lev. 1:1-2)
The Manual of Sacrifice, Part One (Lev. 1:3—6:7)
The Manual of Sacrifice, Part Two (Lev. 6:8—7:38)
The Inauguration of Israel's Worship (Lev. 8:1—10:20)
The Manual of Purification (Lev. 11:1—16:34)
The Law of Holiness (Lev. 17:1—26:46)
The Commutation of Vows and Tithes (Lev. 27:1-34)
The Preparation for Pilgrimage (Num. 1:1—10:10)
The Departure from Sinai (Num. 10:11-28)

In the Wilderness: Israel's Pilgrimage to the Land of Promise. Numbers 10:29—21:35

A Guide for the Wilderness (Num. 10:29-32)
The Ark of the Lord (Num. 10:33-36)
Murmuring at Taberah (Num. 11:1-3)
Craving at Kibroth-hattaavah (Num. 11:4-35)
The Revolt of Miriam and Aaron (Num. 12:1-16)
The Failure to Enter the Promised Land (Num. 13:1—14:45)
A Collection of Material on Ritual Observances (Num. 15:1-41)
The Rebellion of Korah (Num. 16:1-50)
The Divine Sign of the Election of the Levites (Num. 17:1-13)
The Work and Wages of Priests and Levites (Num. 18:1-32)
Purification for Those Who Touch the Dead (Num. 19:1-22)
The Sin of Moses at Meribah (Num. 20:1-13)
Edom Refuses Passage Through Her Land (Num. 20:14-21)
The Death of Aaron (Num. 20:22-29)
Victory Over Arad (Num. 21:1-3)
The Fiery Serpents (Num. 21:4-9)
The Route Around Edom and Moab (Num. 21:10-20)
Victory Over Sihon and Og (Num. 21:21-35)

The Camp in the Plains of Moab: Preparation for Entering the Promised Land. Numbers 22:1—36:13

Balaam and His Oracles Concerning Israel (Num. 22:1—24:25)

COMMENTARY

AT SINAI:
THE ARRANGEMENT OF ISRAEL'S LIFE
AROUND THE HOLY

Leviticus 1:1—Numbers 10:28

Introduction (Lev. 1:1-2)

Leviticus begins in the midst of a narrative sequence (see the Introduction). The scene has been set, the principal characters introduced, and the plot is under way. All this is assumed to be known by the reader of the introductory verses to the first section of Leviticus (1:1-2). "LORD" is the proper name for God in the Old Testament. The name is printed in capitals as in 1:1, when the Hebrew word behind it is YHWH, the sacred Tetragrammaton revealed to Moses (Exod. 3:13-14). It is sometimes written elsewhere "Jehovah," giving it the vowels of the Hebrew word for "lord," as the Jews, out of reverence, had done by New Testament times to avoid speaking the divine name. Here in 1:1 the Lord speaks as the God who has delivered Israel from Egypt and brought them to his holy mount to make covenant with them. The Covenant has been concluded in Exodus 24 and now Israel is being formed for life as the Covenant People.

Israel, of course, is addressed as this Covenant People. They are still in camp at the foot of Sinai. The great revelation of God's will for their life is in progress, emphasized in the repeated formula: "The LORD ... spoke to [Moses] ... saying, 'Speak to the people of Israel, and say to them ...'" Moses, who was introduced in the opening chapters of Exodus, is the mediator of this knowledge of God; throughout Leviticus he is simply and solely the instrument of revelation and appears primarily in the formula.

The Lord speaks "from the tent of meeting." This is the alternate name for the Tabernacle, whose plan and construction have been described in Exodus 25-31, 35-40. It was the portable shrine which Israel carried about with them in the wilderness and erected at each camp site. The name "tent of meeting" grows out of its use as the place of the assembly of the people before God; there they "met" him. At the end of Exodus (40:34-38) the cloud which had appeared on the top of Sinai during the making of the Covenant to manifest the presence of God moved to the Tabernacle. Now the Lord speaks with Moses "from the tent of meeting" rather than from the summit of Sinai.

The material in Leviticus 1:1—Numbers 10:28 is held together within the framework of the narrative about what was revealed to Israel at Sinai. It is the continuation of the account of Israel's being made the Covenant People of the Lord which began in Exodus 19. More strictly it is the remainder of P's Sinai narrative, which began at Exodus 24:16. The place of God's presence as the Holy One in the midst of Israel has been created in the Tabernacle sequence; Leviticus and the first part of Numbers now tell how Israel's life is to be arranged around the Holy as its defining center. His presence is henceforth the sovereign focus of Israel's existence, and all that they do must be a response to God's nature and will. So there comes in Leviticus that sequence of instructions concerning Israel's religion: how she is to conduct her cultic and moral commerce with the Holy God whose presence the Tabernacle enshrines and manifests.

The Manual of Sacrifice (Lev. 1:3—7:38)

The first matter to be dealt with after the erection of the Tabernacle was the worship of the Lord through sacrifice. How shall Israel offer itself in adoration, gratitude, and confession to the Holy God? How shall communion with God be actualized in the form of worship? How shall the repentance of men and the forgiveness of God be joined across the chasm separating the visible human and invisible divine realms? The "manual of sacrifice" is one answer to these questions, and it is placed here to show its significance in Israel's faith. So God now speaks to Moses concerning the offerings which are to be brought to the Tabernacle and sacrificed on the great altar of burnt offering which stood in its court (Exod. 27:1-8).

In Leviticus 1:3—7:38 there are two sections (1:3—6:7 and 6:8—7:38), each of which deals with the same five offerings. In both, the instructions are primarily concerned with the "how" of the ritual of sacrifice. The "why" and "when" come seldom to the fore except in the case of the sin and the guilt offerings.

Faced with this seeming preoccupation with external techniques, the interpreter is left to search out the available clues to the meaning of each sacrifice, remembering that sacrifice has the larger context of many other passages in the Old Testament and the whole faith of the Old Testament concerning the Lord. The external techniques are not ends in themselves; they are the public and visible expression of concern for the profounder significant realities which lie behind and within the ritual.

In these chapters the practice of bringing offerings and sacrifice is not so much originated as regulated and incorporated into the official cult of Israel. Certainly Israelites had practiced sacrifice in various ways since the time of the fathers. But here those offerings which had a particularly prominent role in the ritual of the Covenant People are identified and controlled with specific instruction about how they are to be presented as offerings *to the Lord*. Leviticus 1:3—7:38 is not a history of the origin and development of sacrifice. Rather it is the divine provision for the religious economy of old Israel, so that offerings may be used to accomplish the necessities of praise and fellowship and reconciliation required by the Covenant relationship. It is the ordering of these offerings according to the Lord's will, so that the ritual may be peculiarly and particularly appropriate as Israel's worship of the Lord.

Nor is this passage an account of every kind of offering which was practiced in Israel (for example, the sacrifices associated with the Feasts of Passover and First Fruits are not included). Nor does it represent all the various ways in which offerings were made throughout Israel's religious history. These texts represent rather the final stage of a long development as it reached its culmination in the ritual of the postexilic Temple in Jerusalem. They result from priestly effort to standardize and schematize the offering of those sacrifices of primary importance in public worship in Judah; and as concerns their literary history, they belong to the strand of material called the Priestly document. They are not part of the basic Priestly narrative but have been inserted in it between Exodus 40 and Leviticus 8. The two sections (1:3—6:7 and 6:8—7:38) have different backgrounds; the first is presupposed by the second, which adds to and extends its regulations. When the text attributes its contents to Moses as the recipient of the Lord's instruction, it does so for two reasons. First, from the time of Moses and the Covenant of Sinai all cultic prac-

tice was conducted within the authority and meaning of the Covenant, and therefore whatever developed was "Mosaic." Second,
putting within the Sinai and wilderness period all normative material which bore on Israel's religion was an interpretative theological procedure followed by Israel's earliest theologians. By
bringing every instruction and institution into the environment of
Sinai they were bearing witness that all was founded on and was an
implementation of the will of the Lord, who there made covenant with them.

Of course, sacrificial ritual was not peculiar to Israel. It was
common to all the peoples around Israel and belonged to the
old pre-Mosaic Semitic stock of religious practices. While the
Israelites brought some forms of sacrifice into Canaan when the
land was conquered (for example, the Passover), they also took
over elements of the ritual of Canaan for their own use. Ancient
cuneiform texts (discovered at Ras Shamra) tell of Canaanite
rituals which had some features in common with those of Israel.
Some of the technical names for sacrifices are the same. This
demonstrates the antiquity of many of Israel's sacrifices, and
shows some relation between Israel and Canaan in cultic matters.

But the significant thing for Israel was not merely the fact of
sacrifice, but *to whom* it was made and what relation it effected
between God and people. Israel never adopted without adapting;
she could not, because the dynamic and imperious uniqueness of
her jealous God penetrated her every religious form and infused
each with a character more appropriate to his nature. At the
heart of all sacrifice lies the instinctively felt need on the part of
ancient man to recognize the presence and power of the gods. In
Israel the pagan instinct is acknowledged as valid, and is claimed
and cleansed. God accepts and orders sacrifice as an access to
himself, an acceptable way of communication with him. What
makes it valid is nothing inherent in the procedure of sacrifice,
but first of all the will of God that it should be valid, and second
the integrity and correctness of the intention with which it is
brought. The crucial point beyond all others is that sacrifice in
old Israel was *to the Lord*. All was directed and devoted to the
God of Sinai and the Covenant, to the one true God in distinction from all the gods worshiped in other cults. Thus sacrifice was
an instrument of the monotheistic current in Israel; it was a witness to the God who alone was true God; it was a way of devot-
ing self to him. The priest's meticulous care about the exact,

proper technique for the ritual was an expression of Israel's concern that the offering be presented exclusively to the Lord according to his will.

Study of the five types of sacrifice dealt with in Leviticus 1:3—7:38 shows that they cannot all be interpreted according to any one idea of the meaning of sacrifice. In the biblical period several meanings were associated with sacrifice, among which three stand out in particular. Some offerings were brought as gifts; they were acts of adoration, thanksgiving, and devotion. Some, like the peace offering, centered in communion; in them the worshiper entered into the fellowship of a meal with God, with whom his relation was strengthened and renewed. Still others were designed for the circumstances in which the relationship with God was disturbed by sin, and were means of acknowledging sin in confession, presenting what God deemed acceptable for atonement (at-one-ment), and receiving his forgiveness.

Neither in the synagogue nor in the church is the ritual of animal or grain sacrifice performed any more. In both cases this is due to a historical event. For the Jews it is because the Temple was destroyed and desecrated and the Jews excluded, first by the Romans, then the Muslims. Since sacrificial ritual could be carried out only in the Jerusalem Temple, the ritual has ceased to this day among the Jews. What the Jews would do were the Temple site to fall into their hands again is a matter of dispute among them. The Church does not carry on sacrifice. In the life of Jesus Christ and its consecration in death, the meaning and purpose of sacrifice in the Israel of God is fulfilled and accomplished once for all, and the believer enters into the work of his death by faith. What the believer reads in the Old Testament description of sacrifice is a testimony to the work done for him in his Savior. The Word here speaks concerning our nature, the desperate need which afflicts us in our existence before God, and the arrangement by God instituted in preliminary fashion in Israel, by which we may offer ourselves to God. "In these sacrifices there is a reminder of sin year after year" (Heb. 10:3).

So sacrifice as ritual transaction to be performed, with animal and grain offerings, has been done away with in the Church. It has come to an end, but not because sacrifice has no meaning for the Church or place in our relationship to God. It has its end, and therefore its goal and true interpretation, in Jesus Christ. Whenever the Christian rejoices in the theme "Christ in our

place," he takes up the language and meaning of sacrifice as
sacrament, sacrifice as the way God encounters us sinners. In and
through Christ we adore and thank God, have our true communion with him, offer our repentance, and receive his forgiveness. He,
Christ, is our at-one-ment with God. In these Old Testament passages we are taught what work God does in his Son for his people.
The only sacrifice left for Christians to offer is the one for which
Paul appeals in Romans 12:1: ". . . your bodies as a living sacrifice, holy and acceptable to God, which is your spiritual worship."

The Manual of Sacrifice, Part One: Instructions for the Ritual of Offerings (Lev. 1:3—6:7)

how to

The first table of instructions concerning offerings covers the
burnt offering, cereal offering, peace offering, sin offering, and
guilt offering. The content of the whole is terse, objective, and
stylized; it is a fabric of repeated formulas, varied in each case
to allow for the different sacrifice or animal under consideration.
The divisions within the section on each offering are arranged
according to the animal or kind of cakes being presented, or
(in the case of the sin and guilt offerings) according to the offerer
or the occasion. The section is addressed to the people, and its
formal style seems suited for public instruction of the laity concerning the different rituals of offering.

In the descriptions of each ritual some items recur constantly;
the comment will deal first with these recurring features. These
are concerned with:

The object offered. In the animal sacrifice, the offering may be
a bull, sheep, or goat; turtledoves or young pigeons are allowed
for those who cannot afford the more expensive animal. The
cereal offering always consists of fine flour, frankincense, and oil.
A male animal has place of preference, but in certain cases a
female is permitted and even specified. Always the animal must
be "without blemish," an offering of honor and reverence, the
best for the Lord. (See the specifications concerning the conditions of animals for sacrifice in Leviticus 22:17-33.) In the animal sacrifices, fat and blood are of particular importance. Except in the burnt offering, when the entire animal is consumed,
it is the fat and fatty organs which are burnt on the altar. The
blood is always subject to a particular treatment. In most cases
it is splashed against the base of the altar. In the sin offering a

part of the blood is sprinkled on the curtain of the inner sanctuary, and another part smeared on the horns of the altar of incense. (On the special function of blood in sacrifice, see Leviticus 17:10-13.) In the cereal offering the use of leaven and honey is prohibited; salt is required.

The laying on of hands. The one who brings animal sacrifice lays his hand on the head of the offered animal in presenting it at the Tabernacle. The purpose of this ritual is not a mechanical conveying of one's sins, making the animal an external substitute in place of the offerer. It is rather a way of identifying oneself with the sacrifice, so that the offerer is personally involved by intention and devotion in what is done to and through the sacrifice. It becomes his own surrender to God for the purpose for which the offering is brought.

Aaron's sons, the priests. The Aaronic priesthood of the Second Temple in the postexilic period are alone qualified to preside over the ritual of sacrifice. As the elect of God to serve him in the Temple, they act in his name, and their declaratory pronouncements by which the sacrifice is accepted and judged accomplished have divine authority. They do not act as though in the ritual man is doing something to and for a passive God, but rather represent God so that he is active in the sacrifice as the One who permits and achieves the purpose for which the sacrifice was brought.

The altar. At the door of the Tent stood the great altar of burnt offering, the prototype of the ones in the courts of the Solomonic and the postexilic Temples. On it were offered all sacrifices burned with fire (see its description in Exod. 27:1-8).

The expression, "an offering by fire, a pleasing odor to the Lord," had its origin in very early times in a primitive concept of sacrifice, when it was thought that the very odor of the burning sacrifice smelled good to the gods and put them in a mood to be favorable. Here and elsewhere in the Old Testament the crass meaning has clearly gone, and the phrase has become a stylized, archaic expression used as a declaratory formula of the priest to pronounce the offering as satisfactory; that is, God accepts it for the purpose for which it was brought. Paul uses a turn of the same phrase in Philippians 4:18 concerning gifts sent to him, and in Ephesians 5:2 concerning Christ's sacrifice.

The expression, "make atonement for," is used as a concluding formula to state the effect of the sin and guilt offerings. It is

used only once of another sacrifice, the burnt offering (1:4), and
there it carries its most general sense of strengthening a relationship. In the offerings occasioned by sin it has real place, for in
them the reason for the sacrifice is a damaged personal relationship between God and people when the sacred order of the
Covenant has been broken. The meaning of the term in earlier
pre-Israelite times is uncertain: whether it meant "to cover sin"
and so to hide it, or "to wipe it away," implying a physical notion of sin as a stain. But in the Old Testament, and especially
in the Priestly tradition, "make atonement for" is a fixed technical
term of ritual which means "to bring about an expiation." The
sacrifice of which the formula is used makes amends to God for
the sin for which it is brought. The offering for sin and guilt
is not a mechanical or magical procedure which externalizes sin
and depersonalizes its problem. It might, and did, become that
in the eyes of Israel. But that was not its intention, and such
conceptions were denounced by the prophets. Sacrifice to atone
for sin was an ordinance provided by God to establish a means
of reconciliation. It was a way to offer his mercy to those sinners
who would acknowledge their sin and seek the restoration of unity
with God. It should not be forgotten that the expression usually
has the added phrase, "and he shall be forgiven." Forgiveness,
the personal healing of broken relations, is what the sacrifice
conveys.

The Burnt Offering (1:3-17)

The description of how the burnt offering is to be offered is
divided into three sections, which deal with different kinds of
offerings: from the herd (vss. 3-9), from the flock (vss. 10-13),
and an offering of birds (vss. 14-17). The Hebrew name for the
sacrifice means "that which goes up," that is, ascends by fire
and smoke to God. The genius of this sacrifice is that it is wholly
burnt on the altar, the entire animal being consumed as an offering to God. It is a gift offering, presented to please the King of
Heaven. The offerer by bringing it shows his gratitude, faith,
and adoration. He brings the burnt offering "that he may be
accepted before the LORD" (vs. 3). This does not mean that the
sacrifice is the condition of any relationship at all to the Lord,
or the means of joining the Covenant People to him. It is rather
a means of strengthening the relation which already pertains. By
it God is glorified in an act of personal adoration, as a human

king is honored by the gift of one who is admitted to his presence. When it is said that the sacrifice is "to make atonement for
him" (vs. 4), the term must be understood in its most general
sense: "bringing more closely together in the harmony of favor."
The disrupted relationship presupposed by the sin and guilt offering is not the circumstance here. The existing tie between God
and faithful man is renewed and maintained.

The Cereal Offering (2:1-16)

The Hebrew word for this sacrifice in general usage means a
"gift," a present offered to express reverence, thanks, homage,
or allegiance. In other parts of the Old Testament the word can
refer both to animal and grain offerings, but in the Priestly tradition it is used, as it is here, exclusively for offerings of grain. In
actual practice it was usually brought in conjunction with an animal sacrifice, most frequently the burnt offering.

The cereal offering was made up of fine flour, oil, and frankincense, and could be presented uncooked, or prepared in a variety of ways. It was always to include "the salt of the covenant,"
the symbolic ingredient of binding and perpetual unity (2:13;
see Num.18:19; II Chron. 13:5). The use of leaven and honey
(a thick syrup prepared from grapes) was forbidden because
both, having fermented ingredients, were to the Hebrew mind
symbolical of corruption. The offering had to represent a sincere
and willing commitment, uncorrupted by deceit or dishonest
intent.

The priests had a right to part of the cereal offering. The part
placed on the altar to be burnt was called "its memorial portion"
(2:9), a term which indicates the purpose of the offering; it
served to bring the worshiper to God's gracious remembrance. It
is the ritual counterpart of the numerous Old Testament prayers
that God "remember" his Covenant, people, and devotees, an
equivalent of another Old Testament formula of prayer, "to call
on the name of the LORD."

The Peace Offering (3:1-17)

The description of the peace offering falls into three sections
dealing with the way in which sacrifices from the herd (vss. 1-5),
from the flock (vss. 6-11), or of a goat (vss. 12-17) are to be
offered. The ritual prescribed is much the same as that for the
burnt offering, except that here only part of the animal is con-

sumed by fire—the fat and some of the bodily organs. The rest
is reserved to be eaten by the offerer and the priests. Therein lies
the distinctiveness of the sacrifice. The portion burned on the
altar is "food offered by fire to the LORD." The ritual provides
a meal which the Lord as chief and honored participant shares
with people and priest.

The qualifying name of the sacrifice, "peace," is a derivation
of a Hebrew term which means "wholeness," "harmony," or
"well-being." Here the communion motif is dominant. In the
sharing of the meal, the unity and integrity of God's fellowship
with his Covenant People are expressed and strengthened. That
fellowship, when it was unbroken and harmonious, meant health
and peace for the soul that shared it. The Covenant at Sinai was
instituted by a sacred meal shared by the elders of Israel and
God (Exod. 24:9-11), and every observance of the peace offering could mean a renewal of the well-being which the Covenant
brought and offered.

Since the actual eating lay outside the sphere of priestly ritual,
it is not described in these particular regulations; it was presupposed as the consummation and center of the sacrifice.

The Sin Offering (4:1—5:13)

This sacrifice has a particular prominence in the priestly system. Following the Exile and the impact of its tragedy as judgment on the conscience of Israel, the ritual of the Second Temple
concentrated more and more on those rites which dealt with sin
and which worked atonement where the relationship between
God and his Covenant People had been disrupted. The description of the ritual of the sin offering has four principal sections,
each describing how the sacrifice is to be performed for certain
individuals or groups: for the anointed priest (4:1-12), for the
whole congregation of Israel (4:13-21), for a ruler (4:22-26),
and for one of the common people (4:27—5:13). The last section provides for a scaled variety of sin offerings according to
what the laity could afford: a goat (4:27-31), a lamb (4:32-35),
two turtledoves or pigeons (5:7-10), or a portion of fine flour
(5:11-13). In 5:1-6 there is a list of typical situations in which
the sin offering is to be brought.

When the sin offering is an animal, the entire sacrifice is not
consumed on the altar. Only the fat and certain bodily organs
are burnt there; the rest is carried "outside the camp" to a clean

place to be burnt. The treatment of the blood is distinctive. The priest performs a particular ritual, besprinkling the curtain of the Holy of Holies seven times, so that the blood is consecrated and accepted by the Lord to do the work of atonement. Then blood is smeared also on the horns of the altar of incense before the rest is poured at the base of the altar of burnt offering.

The general introduction to each section of the sin offering specifies that the ritual is to be used only for unwitting or inadvertent sins. This would seem to restrict the application of the sin offering to cases of sin by mistake, to commandments broken in ignorance or innocently. Such cases would most likely be infractions of the ritual regulations, especially those applying to the uncleanness which would disqualify a person from participation in the services of the Temple. Certainly the majority of cases were of this type. But the list of typical cases for which the sin offering was to be brought (5:1-6) includes, along with ritual uncleanness, social and personal failures as well: failure to serve as a witness when obligated, rashly sworn oaths. Unwitting sins as a classification meant something more than sins committed in ignorance; they probably included sins of weakness, the evil a man practices when he would not (see Rom. 7:17-20). What the term means to exclude is the sin committed "with a high hand," the disobedience which is premeditated, intentional, and of a set purpose (Num. 15:30-31).

The sin offering is not a device by which a man deals with his own sin. The ritual is provided and ordered by God. The cultic actor is the anointed priest, divinely chosen to represent God in dealings with his people. The offerer brings the sacrifice as acknowledgment that he has sinned; it is his public confession and turning to God. In the sacrifice the priest makes atonement for him and he is forgiven. The sin offering is an instrument of mercy and grace, God's offer of forgiveness to those who are repentant and who seek at-one-ment with him against whom is every sin.

The Guilt Offering (5:14—6:7)

The functional distinction between the guilt offering and the sin offering is not clear at every point, and it is difficult to know from the present text when one instead of the other was used. In the guilt offering only an unblemished ram was allowed, and it had to be of a specified value, reckoned according to the shekel of the Temple. Moreover, restitution had to accompany the guilt offering; it was given either to the priest for the Lord or to the person who had been wronged. In a later section (7:1-10) something about the actual ritual is said; except for the use of the blood, the procedure is like that for the sin offering.

This section is arranged in three parts which describe different occasions for bringing the guilt offering. It is to be brought: by those who sin "unwittingly" (for this expression see comment on the sin offering) in the matter of "the holy things of the LORD," that is, those who violate any consecration of gifts or tithes or vows (5:14-16); by those who suspect or fear that they may have broken a commandment, but are not certain (5:17-19); by those who have acted unfaithfully toward the Lord by wronging their neighbor in money or property matters (6:1-7). Since there are laws which state the punishment for these violations (Exod. 22:7-15), the offering is for those who of their own initiative confess these sins and make restitution.

The guilt offering also makes atonement for the guilty before the Lord and conveys the Lord's forgiveness to him. Numbers 5:6-7 says specifically that confession is to accompany the guilt offering.

The Manual of Sacrifice, Part Two: Further Instructions for Offerings to the Lord (Lev. 6:8—7:38)

In this second section the same five offerings are again treated, though the order is different; here the sacrifice of peace offerings comes last. Each division begins with the formula, "This is the law of . . ." The instructions are directed to Aaron and his sons and so are meant particularly for the priests; however, the instructions for the peace offering lack the address to the priests because this sacrifice involved the laity also in the ritual of eating. The material in this second table contains additional instructions concerning the ritual techniques to be followed in dealing with the various sacrifices. It is, on the whole, Priestly material concerning the disposal of the offering, specifying what part belongs to the priest. The dominant motif is care for "the holy," that which has become consecrated to ordained use.

The Law of the Burnt Offering (6:8-13)

This law provides that the fire on the altar of burnt offering shall be kept perpetually alight. The morning sacrifice is to be kindled from the fire which has burned since the evening sacrifice was offered. The aroma of praise thus goes up constantly from the Temple, and Israel is never without the sacrament of adoration in its midst.

The Law of the Cereal Offering (6:14-23)

The portion of the cereal offering which is to be reserved for the officiating priests and the manner in which it is to be eaten so as to respect its character as holy to the Lord are specified in this section. Verses 19-23 record instructions given Moses concerning the cereal offering to be brought by Aaron on the day when he is anointed, that is, installed in office. It is the continuing obligation of those who succeed Aaron as the anointed priest. The cereal offering of the priests is consumed wholly on the altar; no portion of it is eaten.

The Law of the Sin Offering (6:24-30)

The disposition of that part of the sacrifice not burnt on the altar is controlled by this law. "It is most holy," and therefore is to be eaten only in the precincts of the Tabernacle and by the priests alone. All that comes in contact with it becomes holy and must be treated ritually. If the blood of the sin offering is used to perform the sprinkling ritual before the Holy of Holies, none of the sacrificed animal may be eaten; this would apply on the Day of Atonement and in the two rituals described in 4:3-21.

The Law of the Guilt Offering (7:1-10)

In the matters which it treats, this law is the same as that for the sin offering. That offering also is "most holy" and the parts of it not burnt are reserved for the priests, to be eaten in the Holy Place. Verses 2-5 give instructions about the ritual of the guilt offering which did not appear in 5:14-16. The blood is thrown round about the base of the altar; the fat and certain fatty organs are burnt.

The Law of the Peace Offering (7:11-38)

This section is made up of further specifications for the peace offering (vss. 11-18), and a series of regulations dealing with its eating, necessary because of the character of the peace offering as a meal (vss. 19-36).

In 7:11-18 there are listed the functions of the peace offering:

it may be presented as a thank offering, a votive offering, or a freewill offering. The thank offering is a sacrifice brought in gratitude to acknowledge the help and blessing of the Lord in sickness, adversity, or other trouble. With it are to be brought three kinds of unleavened cakes for offering to God, and one kind that is leavened for eating in the sacrificial meal. One of each kind goes to the priest as an "offering" removed and reserved for the clergy. All the flesh of the animal must be eaten on the day of the sacrifice. A peace offering may also be a votive offering (a sacrifice brought in fulfillment of a vow, often made conditional on the fulfillment of prayer), or a freewill offering (a sacrifice brought in spontaneous praise and adoration or in hope of future help). In these two cases the meal may continue a second day, but not a third, lest the meat become spoiled and so be an abomination, rejected by the Lord as unfit.

Verses 19-21 contain the regulations dealing with the problem of clean and unclean (see Lev. 11-16) in eating the peace offering. Meat which becomes unclean is not to be used, nor are unclean persons to partake. Violation of the regulations leads to excommunication from the religious community.

Verses 22-27 prohibit the eating of fat specified for ritual use, and the eating of blood. Both were considered taboo because of their special role in cultic procedures (see 3:16-17; 17:10-14). Violation of these prohibitions leads to excommunication.

Verses 28-36 specify the portions of the peace offering which go to the priests. The breast and right thigh are the perpetual due of the officiating clergy as their share in the feast. The breast is subject to a peculiar ritual; it is "waved," that is, moved to and fro before the Holy Place, to show that it is consecrated to the Lord and yet is returned to the priests; it is therefore called a "wave offering."

Verses 37-38 are a conclusion to this section, repeating the introductory phrase, "this is the law."

The Inauguration of Israel's Worship (Lev. 8:1—10:20)

In Leviticus 8:1—10:20 the Aaronic family is ordained to be priests in Israel, sacrificial worship is inaugurated in the Tabernacle through Aaron's ministry, and the first problem in the conduct of the priesthood emerges in the sin of Nadab and Abihu.

The narrative covering these matters is a direct sequel to the closing chapters of Exodus, where the Tabernacle is completed and filled by the glory of the Lord. In Exodus the instructions for ordination of the priesthood were given, but they were not carried out. In Leviticus 8:1-36 the basic narrative resumes to complete the story of how Israel's entire system of worship was ordained and founded at Sinai. The manual of offerings in Leviticus 1-7 appears between Exodus 40 and Leviticus 8 because instructions concerning the five types of offerings to be brought to the Tabernacle are presupposed in the ritual of Leviticus 8-10.

The priesthood is the central theme of these chapters. They tell how the office of the priest was instituted by God as part of the founding of Israel's religion. The priest, along with the prophet and king, made up that trilogy of offices through which the personal relation between God and people was effected and maintained. The sphere of the priest was the authorized shrine where God willed to be present so that the people might appear before him. The role of the priest was quite broad and by no means restricted to the offering of sacrifice. Originally his most important task was inquiring after the will of God and giving the people God's instruction. He learned and passed on the tradition of faith, remembering and maintaining for the whole people the knowledge of God's acts of revelation and the declarations of his will. The priest also accepted the confessions of sin through sacrifice and proclaimed God's forgiveness. He officiated at the rites of blessing and cursing. He distinguished between the holy and profane and between the clean and unclean, so as to maintain the sanctification of the people, keeping them in subjection to God's holiness. He presided over their stewardship and thanksgiving. When certain legal cases were brought to the shrine, he declared God's decision concerning them. Although the priest suffers by comparison with the prophet in our notion about biblical religion, the faith of Israel would be unthinkable without his work.

In Leviticus 8:1—10:20 it is the household of Aaron which is ordained, and the members of this family alone are viewed as eligible to be priests. This is not the position of Deuteronomy, where the entire tribe of Levi has the priestly office. Nor does it represent the situation in early Israel and the patriarchal period when heads of families performed priestly rites. In Israel's history certain groups seem always to have been recognized as

especially qualified to be priests. But the restriction of priesthood
to Aaron and his house is a peculiarity of the P tradition, and the
circumstances of these chapters belong to the latest monarchial
period and the time of the Second Temple. Behind them lies a long-
developing history which is not fully reported in the Old Testament. The theological intention of these chapters is to declare
that the priesthood exercised by Aaron's family is an ordinance
of God, belonging by his will to the religion which was founded
at Sinai and indispensable for maintaining the Covenant relationship instituted there between God and people.

The Church reads here of the office assumed by Jesus, who is
the "high priest of our confession" (Heb. 3:1). Not only are these
chapters a report of one part of the history of our faith, but they
also describe the role into which Jesus entered in his death and
resurrection (Heb. 4:14—10:39). In him we have a High Priest
who is holy, blameless, unstained, separated from sinners, exalted
above the heavens. He is High Priest forever. He entered once for
all into the Holy Place, taking his own blood to secure our eternal
redemption and to purify our consciences from dead works to
serve the living God. By his assumption of the office, the use and
need of priests as religious officers is at an end. Now the believer
is made able to do himself what only the priest could do: "enter
the sanctuary" and "draw near" to God (Heb. 10:19, 22). The
fulfillment of the office of priest by the crucified Jesus has brought
the priesthood of all believers into existence.

The Ordination of the Priests (8:1-36)

In Exodus 29:1-37 Moses was given instructions by God concerning the ordination of Aaron and his sons to be the priests of
the Tabernacle, the ministers of the Lord at his sanctuary. Leviticus 8 describes the execution of the instructions, in words almost
identical with the earlier chapter. In the ritual of ordination Moses
is in charge; in the authority of his own role as the mediator of
God's Covenant will for Israel he conducts priestly rites, for
which Aaron and his sons are qualified only by the service of
ordination. The entire ritual is celebrated to show that the Aaronic
priesthood is an institution of God, existing by his will and meant
to serve his purpose. Neither Aaron nor his sons after him were
ready to be priests apart from what was done in the ordination:
as sinners they needed atonement, as common men they had to be
consecrated and set aside, as ordinary men they had to be en-

dowed. Ultimately this ritual of ordination is an act of God whereby men are set in the place of service as priests.

The ritual begins (vss. 1-4) "at the door of the tent of meeting," for Aaron is not yet qualified to enter. All the requisite items to be used in the service are brought, and the congregation is assembled. Because the ordination involves them and commits them to Aaron's priestly office, they must witness and believe in what is done.

The first part of the service (vss. 5-13) is a ritual of induction. Aaron was washed to cleanse him for his work in the holy place. He was clad in the garments (prepared in Exod. 28) which symbolized his endowment with the capacities of the priesthood. Then he was consecrated by an anointing which set him aside for this peculiar work. As a part of the ceremony the Tabernacle and all that was in it were anointed, so that the person and the place of the priestly function were consecrated together. Aaron's sons were washed and vested, but not anointed.

The ordination service was completed by three offerings of sacrifice performed according to the pertinent regulations in Leviticus 1-7, but with peculiar features appropriate to the occasion. A bull was brought as a sin offering (vss. 14-17) to make atonement for Aaron and his sons and for the altar of burnt offering (see Lev. 4). This was followed by a ram of burnt offering (vss. 18-21) offered on behalf of Aaron and his sons (see Lev. 1). Then a second ram was offered (vss. 22-29) according to the ritual of the sacrifice of peace offering (see Lev. 3; 7:11-18); it was called "the ram of ordination" and was to be eaten as a meal of communion (vss. 31-32), shared with the Lord. A final act of consecration was performed as Aaron and his sons in their vestments were sprinkled with a mixture of anointing oil and blood from the altar (vs. 30). Then they were commanded to wait at the door of the tent until their seven days of ordination were complete (vss. 33-36).

The Inauguration of the Priestly Ministry (9:1-24)

In the events of this chapter, the establishment of a way of worship designed to manifest the presence of the Lord in the midst of Israel reaches its climax. Here Aaron and his sons enter into that ministry for which they were ordained and for which the entire Tabernacle with all its equipment was prepared. Here the Lord appears to Israel through his glory to manifest his pres-

ence and to accept their relation to him through the ministry of
the priesthood. A dramatic and awesome sign is granted, by which
Israel's worship is validated and consecrated.

On the eighth day, after the seven days of Aaron's ordination
(8:33) are complete, Moses commands the priests and the elders
(representing the congregation) to initiate the service of sacrifice.
Aaron and his sons are to offer a separate sin offering and burnt
offering for them and for the people, and then a sacrifice of peace
offering for the whole group. A cereal offering was burnt with the
people's burnt offering. Thus one of each of the types of offering
was used in this initial service. (The guilt offering was omitted,
possibly because of the close similarity to the sin offering and its
specialized function. On the five types and the technique for their
offering, see Leviticus 1-7.) The sin offering comes first to show
in what condition both priests and people must appear before
God's presence; they are alike sinners, and atonement for both is
the inevitable necessity for a relation to the Holy God. Then come
the burnt offering and the sacrifice of peace offering in such order
as to exhibit confession, devotion, and communion as the proper
rhythm by which Israel draws near to the God who by his own
gracious condescension comes to them and dwells in their midst.

When the offerings are completed, Aaron performs another of
the priestly duties: he lifts up his hands toward the people and
blesses them (vs. 22). Using such words as the Aaronic blessing
given in Numbers 6:22-27, the priest by God's authority puts
God's name on the people and declares over them God's good will
and help. Thus he extends the original "blessing" given first to
Abraham and belonging as an inheritance to all who are the
chosen of God. Then for the first time, Aaron is introduced by
Moses into the Tent of Meeting, the place of God's presence.
Then, and only then, is the ordination of Aaron and the inauguration of Israel's worship complete. The priest standing on behalf
of the people and for them is admitted to the very presence of
God.

The entire service was performed in tense expectation of a
great climax promised at its beginning: "Today the LORD will
appear to you" (vs. 4). When Moses and Aaron return from
within the Tent and together bless the people a second time, a
mighty and dread sign is given: "The glory of the LORD appeared
to all the people," and divine fire consumed the portions of the
sacrifice still burning on the altar. The phrase "the glory of the

LORD" here means the luminous unearthly brilliance by which the Lord showed his presence. The glory of the Lord had descended from Sinai into the Tabernacle when it was completed (Exod. 40:34-38); here the glory is shown to the people that they may know that the Lord truly meets them and accepts them in the worship which he has ordained. A sacrifice burnt by divine fire appears elsewhere in the Old Testament as a sign that God accepts those who offer it (see Judges 6:21; I Kings 18:38; I Chron. 21:26). When all the people saw the sign they knew that God had met them and was pleased with their worship; they shouted and fell on their faces in awe and joy.

The Sin of Nadab and Abihu (10:1-20)

The ordination of Aaron and his sons to be priests is hardly finished when two of them, Nadab and Abihu, fail in the exercise of priesthood and are punished by the Lord. This incident and the consequences drawn from it serve to demonstrate the solemn responsibility of the priests in their ministry before the Holy God.

Nadab and Abihu erred in bringing unholy (literally, "strange" or "improper") fire before the Lord. The exact nature of the sin is not clarified by the text. In some way they violated the ritual order by which God was to be approached and did what the Lord had not commanded. What matters is that their act was either heedless presumption or carelessness in their priestly ministry. They were struck down by the same divine fire (9:24) which, as a sign of approval, had consumed the sacrifice in the ordination service. Aaron and his other two sons were forbidden the rites of mourning for them (loosening their hair and rending their garments), lest they seem to sympathize with their erring kinsmen against the holiness of God. In verse 3 the meaning of the incident is stated as a serious admonition to all priests in all times: those who draw near to the Lord (the priests) must testify to his holiness by their reverent fear and obedience, so that the Lord will be glorified among all the people. The attitude of the congregation depends on the character of its ministry, and therefore the priests bear an awesome responsibility in their service to proclaim the holiness of the Lord in all that they do. In the Church, where all believers participate in the priesthood, this admonition speaks in urgency to every Christian.

In verses 8-11 wine and strong drink are forbidden the priests while they perform their duties, lest they be unable to do with precision the work summarized in verses 10 and 11. This summary is one of the classic formulas in the Old Testament by which the priestly function is defined. Priests are to distinguish between what is "holy" and "common" or profane (all that is not consecrated), and between the "unclean" and the "clean." These four categories are fundamental distinctions on which the entire Priestly conception of worship is constructed. (On the basic category "holy," see the comment on Leviticus 17-26; and on the relation of the other categories to holiness, see the comment on Leviticus 11-16.) To the priests is also committed the teaching ministry, a work which probably preceded all others in the history of Israel's priesthood. The priests are to instruct the people in all the statutes of the Lord.

Verses 12-15 continue the theme of reverence for the Holy with instructions concerning *where* the priests may eat those portions of the offerings assigned to them. The cereal offering and burnt offering must be eaten in a holy place; the sacrifice of peace offering may be shared with their families in an unsanctified but clean place.

Verses 16-20 settle the problem of why the goat of the sin offering used in the ordination service (Lev. 9) was not eaten as it ought to have been, since its blood was not carried into the inner part of the sanctuary.

The whole chapter warns against the dangers involved in a priesthood carried out by sinful men, as ministers of the Holy Presence. The priest in Israel is not magically transformed or made divine by his ordination. He remains very human. He must bring his own sin offering and be set about with safeguards to assure that he does not presume upon or desecrate the Holiness of which he is a ministering servant.

The Manual of Purification (Lev. 11:1—16:34)

These chapters are concerned with the problem of the unclean and of the way an Israelite is to be cleansed when he has been contaminated by the unclean. They do not deal with the problem in general by discussing its meaning for faith—that is presupposed. Rather they treat certain specific cases where uncleanness is involved and describe what is to be done: clean and unclean food (ch. 11), a woman's uncleanness at childbirth (ch. 12), the identification of leprosy and its ritual of purification (chs. 13-14), and bodily discharges which make unclean (ch. 15). But some attempt must be made to understand what Israel presupposed about the significance of this problem. Unless we grasp something of what was involved here for Israel's faith, these chapters are likely to seem no more than a forbidding compound of superstition and outworn primitive ritual, with no importance at all for a knowledge of God's revelation.

The terms "clean" and "unclean" have only the remotest connection with their ordinary use today in connection with hygiene and sanitation. Actually, we have no English words which gather up precisely what the Hebrew terms mean; the use of "unclean" is an inefficient convenience. Being "unclean" is a danger in a person's relation to God; it has no reference to germs.

In Leviticus 10:10 the priest is given the task of distinguishing between the holy and the common, and between the unclean and the clean. Chapters 11-15 follow the ordination of the priests (Lev. 8-10) because they deal with this work of distinguishing between clean and unclean. In these chapters the priest is constantly at work examining and deciding into which classification people and things fall, declaring their condition, and performing rites of cleansing under appropriate circumstances. This work is not a peripheral and isolated department of a priest's office; it is crucial for his entire ministry. The life of Israel was arranged around the worship and service of the Covenant God. Being a member of the People of God depended on participation in the worship of the Lord and on eligibility so to participate. When a priest declared someone or something unclean or clean he was deciding about eligibility for participation in or for usefulness in the life of God's people. What was unclean could not be brought into relation to the Holy. In the Priestly theology the Lord was, above all else, holy, so the problem of whether people and things were clean or unclean was a constant and crucial one for every Israelite, since his relation to God was ultimately involved. And it was the responsibility of the priest to watch over this problem, exercising every care to be sure that the status of people and things was known and declared, and using all the resources of the cult to cleanse what was unclean. Leviticus 15:31 states the intention of this work: "Thus you shall keep the people of Israel separate from their uncleanness, lest they die in their uncleanness by defiling my tabernacle that is in their midst."

It will be of help to understand the relationship between the two pairs of opposites given in Leviticus 10:10: Holy—common, clean—unclean. These four are basic concepts by which all existence was interpreted in terms of the central cult and the presence of God, who dwelt in the midst of Israel. The fundamental concept is holiness. God is holy. "Holy" means almost the same as "divine"; it is that characteristic of complete otherness and difference which belongs to God in contrast to all else that exists. (For a further discussion of "holy," see the comment on Leviticus 17-26.) All holiness derives from God; people, places, times, and things are consecrated ("made holy") by his act which dedicates them to his special use and brings them into his sphere. "Common," or "profane," is the term for all the world considered on its own; what is not made holy is profane, common. "Common" covers unclean and clean. That is clean which can be related to the Holy or even made holy. But the unclean is by nature excluded from relation to the Holy. It is what the Hebrews call an "abomination" or a "despised thing"; it is offensive to God; by its very condition it is in opposition to the nature of God. So the pairs are not made up of synonyms; they overlap. Holy and unclean are opposite poles, and the movement is from unclean to clean within the common, and on to the holy beyond the common. The concepts make up a system of understanding by which Israel thinks and acts in the whole problem of sanctification, that of bringing national and individual life into conformity to the nature of God. The system is Israel's way, in her own time, of responding to the exhortation: "For I am the LORD your God; consecrate yourselves therefore, and be holy, for I am holy" (11:44).

A closer look at Leviticus 11-15 may well provoke two further questions. Why were these particular things designated as unclean? Does it not appear that uncleanness is an external physical condition, dealt with by ritual, and having little consequence for the inner moral life?

It is a plain fact that we do not see any national or religious reason why we should not eat pork or why contact with the dead should defile a man. But we would err if we assumed that this ought to have been true or could have been true for old Israel. The particular prohibitions in chapters 11-15 were valid for Israel in her own time because of the real situation in which she was called to be the People of God. In the context in which she struggled after consecration, there were many things which threat-

ened her purity and the clarity of her faith, things which no longer
endanger the People of God in the same form. The reason for
many of the prohibitions lay in the long story of Israel's struggle
with the pagan religions around her. Certain animals were sacred
in the heathen cults, or were totems for other peoples and shrines,
or were associated with demons and evil powers. Guarding the
whole sphere of sex against cultic use was a constant battle for
Israel; making sexual intercourse temporarily defiling very effec-
tively sealed off Israel's cult from the practices of the fertility
cults. Rituals for the dead were prominent in Israel's environment; making the dead unclean robbed that practice of any power
in Israel. Not all the prohibitions can be traced to Israel's religious
polemics against foreign religions; some seem to be remnants of
primitive taboos which preserved a power over the mind of Israel
through the years. Others are based on instinctive or cultural aver-
sions, for which there is no historical or national explanation.
But strange and unreasonable as some of the prohibitions seem to
us, in Israel's time and situation they were all calculated to be a
way of expressing reverence for God's holiness and a discipline to
bring life into conformity to election by the Lord. By these re-
strictions Israel bore witness to the fact that the lordship of God
made a difference in living on the side of purity.

All this should indicate that what seems to us to have been
crassly external and physical was not so for Israel at all. Israel did
not separate spirit and flesh, mind and body. The physical and
the psychic were sides of a unity. Anything that had psychic as-
sociation with evil, or symbolic connection with opposition to the
nature of the Lord, possessed physical power to defile. Israel may
have overdone the materialistic and external side of ritual; but
we have gone so far toward intellectualizing and spiritualizing our
notion of evil that we have lost much of the realism about the
physical which belongs to biblical faith. Nor should we conclude
that just because the rituals of purification were described as external acts they had no inner spiritual significance. When an unclean person washed himself, he showed his own will and hunger
to be clean, to be ready for communion with God. Moreover, because the rituals of cleansing were ordained of God they were
doors opened from the side of holiness; they were help which
God provided to maintain the purity of his people. The ritual
could be seen as a *grace*, entered into with joy because a way had
been provided to regain the cleanness appropriate for the People

of God. As long as the system did not become rigid or separated from consciousness of devotion to God, it was in its time a powerful device to bind the wholeness and reality of life to the vocation of being God's people.

Mention of the rituals of purification reminds us that these chapters are concerned not only with drawing a line between clean and unclean, but also with establishing the way uncleanness is to be overcome. In most cases, purification is accomplished by washing with water, after the lapse of a specified time. When the uncleanness is more severe, washing is followed by bringing a burnt offering and a sin offering to the priest. Two matters ought to be noted here. First, the condition of being unclean is not a static one; the regulations do not draw a permanent line dividing the creation in any final dualism of good and bad, of clean and unclean. The line waves back and forth, depending on individual incidents of defilement and counter-action of the Holy through the ritual to overcome the uncleanness. The frontier is never stable; it is a kind of battle line marking the point of the warfare by which the Holy God is reclaiming his own world. Second, the use of the sin offering as an atoning ritual for uncleanness points to the deep connection in Israel's faith between uncleanness and sin. Sin took many forms besides uncleanness, but uncleanness was not ultimately different from sin. It was that kind of condition which fell upon a man because he was involved in a profane world which did not recognize its true Lord. In old Israel it represented the power of the world or of evil over the individual, quite beyond his own resources and will. It is, in a way, analogous to the New Testament powers and spiritual forces over which Christ wins the victory to set men free.

What happens to the theme of clean and unclean in the faith of the New Testament Church? Clearly it does not disappear in the New Israel, precisely because the problem of the sanctification of the Church in the midst of the world does not disappear. In late Judaism the laws concerning uncleanness were greatly amplified and meticulously observed. Unfortunately a legalism entered the observance of them, so that the rabbis concentrated so much on external ritual uncleanness that the real intention and meaning of the theme was obscured. Judaism was unable to free the concern for purification from its traditional elements of superstition and failed to turn the concern toward the real threats to the purity of God's people.

Jesus and Paul broke through the old practice, captured its intention, and applied it to the new situation of the Messianic community. The threat of uncleanness is linked wholly with the danger of sin. Jesus declared that it is not things outside a man, but man's own evil heart which defiles him (Mark 7:14-23); and Paul echoed the teaching of Jesus in declaring that nothing in the whole world is unclean in itself for those in Christ (Rom. 14:14). In the new age the rites of purification are accomplished in Christ's death and his sacraments. The Christian is cleansed through the Lord's word (John 15:3) and his baptism (Eph. 5: 26). The evil heart of man is cleansed by faith (Acts 15:9). The theme of "clean-unclean" is not eliminated; no impure man has any place in the Kingdom of God (Eph. 5:5). Only the pure in heart will see God (Matt. 5:8). The exhortation, "Be ye holy for I am holy," still sounds over the Church. But the believer knows that his sanctification is accomplished by faith in the cleansing death of Jesus, by which the heart is renewed and devoted in singleness to the praise of God and obedience to him.

The Distinction Between Clean and Unclean Food (11:1-47)

This long list simply identifies the living creatures which in Israel are prohibited as food because they are unclean. No reason is given for the distinctions. Behind this Priestly material there is a long and established tradition which is presupposed; its concern is not with "why" but "what." Some of the creatures may be prohibited because of their sacral role in the pagan religions with which Israel struggled, others because of remnants of long-forgotten taboos. Still others were simply repulsive to Israelite sensitivities. In the postexilic period no rationalization of the classification was attempted. What mattered was a distinctive ordained diet which marked Israel as a people separate unto the Lord.

The categories under which the living creatures are listed are the beasts (vss. 1-8), the fish (vss. 9-12), the birds (vss. 13-19), and the insects (vss. 20-23). A separate category referring to "swarming" (or creeping) things (vss. 29-45)—mostly reptiles— seems to be an addition to the original categories; they make unclean, but were not ordinarily regarded as food. Two sections deal with the uncleanness which comes from touching dead creatures (vss. 24-28, 39-40).

Purification of Women After Childbirth (12:1-8)

In giving birth to a son a woman incurred the same uncleanness
for seven days as in the period of her menstruation (Lev. 15:19-
30). An additional thirty-three days had to pass to complete the
time of her purification. If the child was a girl, both terms were
doubled. After the time of purification the woman was to bring
to the priest a lamb for a burnt offering and a pigeon or turtle-
dove for a sin offering; or, if she was poor, two pigeons or two
turtledoves would do for both.

Leprosy and Its Purification (13:1—14:57)

Of all the conditions which caused uncleanness, leprosy was
by far the most terrible and dramatic. The consequences of being
identified as a leper were drastic; and the rituals for the purification of a leper, if he did recover, were elaborate. This long passage devoted to the subject of leprosy contains two large sections:
one on the symptoms for which the priest is to look in diagnosing
leprosy (13:1-44), and another on the ritual for cleansing a leper
who has gotten well (14:1-32). There are also shorter sections on
leprosy in the fabric of garments (13:47-59) and in the plaster
of houses (14:33-53).

The sections on leprosy in garments and houses raises the
question of what medical condition was comprehended under the
Hebrew word which is translated "leprosy." Clothes and build-
ings do not have leprosy. Nor is the concern only with infection,
but with garments and houses which have the symptoms associated with leprosy. The term certainly covered more than a modern
doctor would diagnose as leprosy, even in its application to hu-
mans. But leprosy was present in ancient Palestine, and the elaborate table of symptoms was broad enough to allow its identification when it appeared.

Leprosy was regarded as a form of uncleanness which was
highly potent and dangerously contaminating. Because of the
virulent contagion of his uncleanness the leper had to go in
mourning (torn clothes and hair unbound), and to cry, "Unclean, unclean," when anyone approached him (13:45-46). He
was put outside the camp to dwell, that is, he was excluded from
the community life of the People of God. This and other references indicate that he was regarded as dead (see Num. 12:12).
Perhaps it was this being reckoned as dead which was the basis

of the opinions about the extreme uncleanness. The leper showed visibly the dissipation of his vitality and the hold of death, which could not be brought in relation to the Living God. He already belonged to the hopeless forbidden realm of death. Leprosy seems to have been regarded at times as a punishment, a smiting of God, and the Hebrew may have felt that all such were marked by God's wrath, whether the reason was known or not.

There was no way in the cult to heal a leper, but when one re-covered from the disease there was an elaborate ritual for his cleansing, particularly designed for his condition. The ritual moved in three stages, based on three aspects of his condition—that he was regarded as dead, unclean, smitten of God. Corre-spondingly he was first readmitted to the camp, then to his own dwelling, and finally to the sanctuary. The rituals for these stages were (1) washing and shaving off all his hair and the ritual of the two birds; (2) washing and shaving again on the seventh day; (3) a guilt offering (sacrificed in a special way), a burnt offering, and a cereal offering, all brought on the eighth day to the priest at the Tent of Meeting. The ritual of the two birds (14:4-7), one slain and the other released, has at least a formal similarity to the ritual of the two goats, of which one was sent away on the Day of Atonement (see Lev. 16). In the guilt offering (Lev. 5:14—6:7 and 7:1-10), the blood is applied to the leper (14:14-18) in a rite similar to that used in the ordination of the priest (Lev. 8:23-24), as though the cleansed man had to be reinducted into the com-munity of God's people.

There is a sense in which the leper's plight illustrates the condi-tion of all of us as we are, apart from the intervention of God; we are subject to death, have no identity in the People of God, and as sinners live under God's wrath with no help in ourselves for our condition. Surely Jesus' cleansing the leper (Mark 1:40-45) carries a message which outruns the miracle involved. The leper testifies to the frustration of the power of the priestly ministry; his uncleanness cannot be reached by its power to claim the man for God. Jesus as the Holy One of God (Mark 1:24) does what no Jew would do—touches the leper, and by his touch holiness vanquishes uncleanness. In him is the help to claim for God every man who is helpless and "outside the camp" of God's people. Through his ministry even the realm of death is invaded, and holiness breaks through into all the spheres of existence lost to God.

Bodily Discharges and Their Purification (15:1-33)

The bodily discharges treated in this chapter are those which come from the normal functioning of sex organs and those caused by disorder or disease. Cases where men are concerned are treated first (vss. 1-18) and then those concerning women (19-30). For monthly menstruation and an emission of semen only washing is required. But where the discharge is irregular, and could be connected with a disease, a burnt offering and a sin offering for atonement are stipulated.

The Day of Atonement (16:1-34)

At the end of the section on purification comes God's instruction to Moses describing what the high priest (Aaron) is to do on the Day of Atonement. In the rites of this one day the priestly responsibility for the relation between Holy God and sinful people reaches its fullest expression. The ritual of this day is the climax and crown of Israel's theology of sanctification, of purification from sin. So crucial did the day become in later Judaism that the rabbis called it "The Day," and devoted an entire book of the Mishnah to its explication. The chapter is introduced (vs. 1) with a reference to Nadab and Abihu, the sons of Aaron, because their death for carelessness in drawing near to God was a dramatic illustration of the tension between the Holy God and a sinful people (see Lev. 10). The Day of Atonement was the focus of God's gracious arrangement whereby this otherwise impossible relationship was renewed and maintained.

The summary at the end of the chapter (vss. 29-34) best describes the general character of the day. It fell on the tenth of Tishri (the seventh month), which was to be observed as a sabbath of solemn rest, when Israel ceased all work and fasted ("afflict yourselves"). Thus the ceremony was kept from being merely a remote observance performed by the priests; the whole people assumed the attitude of attention and contrition. The celebrant was the anointed high priest, the one consecrated to the office of executing the provision God had made in ritual for the people's access to him. The purpose of the rite was to effect a general atonement—for the place of worship (sanctuary, tabernacle, altar), for the priest, and for the people. The regular round of confession and sacrifice initiated by individuals would leave a whole area of sin unresolved. So seriously had Israel come to view sin through the theology of holiness that she felt the land and people and the very shrine itself to be impure and therefore in danger of being unacceptable to God. The Day of Atonement was God's gracious ordinance to cleanse the whole, that is, to make all eligible for dealings with the present Holy One. Once in the year it was to be done.

The sacrificial animals were of two types: those for the sin offering (a bull and two goats), and those for a burnt offering (two rams) after the ritual of sin offering was complete. (On these two kinds of sacrifice, see the comment on Leviticus 1-7.) By the casting of lots one of the goats was assigned to the Lord, the other to "Azazel."

The focal point of the ritual was the entry of the high priest into the Holy of Holies, the innermost chamber of the Tabernacle where the Ark rested in mysterious darkness. Ordinarily he did not go there—only this once in the year. In preparation the priest laid aside his regular priestly attire, washed, and put on the garments of white linen which symbolized purity (Exod. 28:39-43). Then he entered beyond the curtain, first to burn incense before the Ark so that its smoke (a symbol of prayer and adoration) hid the mercy seat. The mercy seat was the empty space above the Ark, between the outstretched wings of the golden cherubim who stood on the cover of the Ark. The Hebrew word for "mercy seat" means "place or means of atonement"; there the Lord condescended to be present and available to Israel (Exod. 25:17-22). It was to the mercy seat that the priest brought the blood of the sin offerings, sprinkling it once against the face of the mercy seat and seven times before it; so the blood with its life, set aside to make atonement, was brought in ritual as near as possible to the Holy Presence. Thereafter, blood was smeared also on the altar of burnt offering to complete the purification of the Tabernacle. By the ritual, Israel and the priest acknowledged their sin and received the atonement of God which removed their impurity.

But the ritual was not yet complete. There remained the goat to be sent away to "Azazel," who is mentioned in the Old Testament only in this chapter and about whose precise identity there is no certainty. But the significance of this part of the ritual is on the whole clear enough. The priest laid his hands on the head of the second goat, confessed the sins of Israel over it, and it was led away into an isolated wilderness from which it could not return. Thus, there were two moments of atonement—the first in the presentation of the blood, the second in the symbolism of the goat who bears away the guilt of Israel. Azazel is surely regarded here as a personal being. He may have originally been a pagan god or demon to whom unorthodox Israelites made sacrifice. When a goat for Azazel was included in the ritual of the Day of Atonement the pagan practice was neutralized by joining it to the worship of the Lord, and Azazel was marked off as evil, the source of sin, and hence the place whither impurity, which had no place in the congregation, could be returned. Azazel appears in later Jewish angelology as one of the minions of Satan.

In the New Testament the ceremony of the Day of Atonement becomes one of the ways to interpret the work of Jesus in his death. Christ fulfills what is here ordained and prepared by God in old Israel as a way of atonement. In him the ritual moment becomes a historical event—atonement is made "once for all." As High Priest, Christ entered the heavenly Sanctuary and, offering his own life through his blood, put away sin (Heb. 9). He is our place and means of atonement. In Leviticus 16 the Church reads of its need for atonement before the presence of the Holy God, understands better the work into which Christ enters in the Cross, and learns how God sets the Son as the propitiation for our sin.

The Law of Holiness (Lev. 17:1—26:46)

The ten chapters of Leviticus running from 17 through 26 contain one of the three large law collections in the Pentateuch. It has, for good reasons, been named "the Holiness Code" or the "Law of Holiness," and is often referred to by the letter "H." It follows the law of clean and unclean and the law for the Day of Atonement, sections which are concerned with the preservation and restoration of the purity of God's people. The primary concern of the law of holiness is to urge the holiness of their God upon the people as a most solemn obligation; they are by their obedience of the Lord's commandments to express his holiness in the ritual and ethical activities of all their life. The repeated theme, "You shall be holy; for I the LORD your God am holy," serves well as a text for the whole.

In its present form H is presented as the speech of the Lord through Moses to the Israelites, or to the priests, or sometimes to both (for example, 17:1-2; 19:1-2). It is set in the great Sinai

narrative as a part of the revelation of God's will to Israel when
the Covenant was established and Israel's worship was founded.
As is the case with a great part of the legal tradition in the Sinai
narrative, its place there is more an affirmation of faith, a theological assertion, than a chronological fact. It is Israel's way of
saying that whatever law she has been given in her history is instruction to implement the original Covenant and comes from the
God who met Israel at Sinai; it is to be understood in this context alone.

The probable date for the collection of H is the middle of the
sixth century B.C.; it seems to have emerged among the exiles in
Babylon, although it is possible that it was collected immediately
before the Exile. It is closely related to Ezekiel, an exilic prophet
who presupposes its existence. It clearly comes earlier than the
main body of the Priestly material and seems to follow Deuteronomy. One speaks of it as a collection because it is not an
original composition. It is rather an edition of legal material already at hand, and contains many smaller units of laws which
had an independent existence and may go far back into Israel's
early religious history. In chapter 19, for instance, there are a
number of little law-series, each dealing with some one specific
concern. When the collection H was incorporated as part of the
Priestly history of Israel's beginnings, it was revised to bring it in
line with the developments which had occurred after worship was
instituted in the Second Temple. Cases of this revision will be
found in chapters 23 and 24.

On first reading, these chapters do not seem to be enough of a
coherent whole to justify calling them a unity. But closer ex-
amination discloses common features of style and intention which
bind them together. The repeated demand that God's holiness be
manifest in the life of his people has already been noted (19:2;
20:7, 8, 26; 21:6, 8, 15, 23). God identifies himself as the Lord
who sanctifies them (20:24; 21:15, 23; 22:9, 16, 32). Over and
over God speaks his own name to cast over the law the absolute
authority of his lordship: "I am the LORD" or "I am the LORD
your God." (As an illustration of the constant use of the sentence, almost like a period, see chapter 19.) The remarkable
distinctiveness of this collection is the passionate urgency with
which it holds holiness before Israel as the essential mark of existence as the People of the Lord. For the law of holiness is not
just a succession of legal rules. It is formulated as a message. It

concludes with a magnificent peroration on the cruciality of keeping the law (ch. 26), and throughout the code the legal form passes into hortatory speech, so that the laws are not only declared but their appeal and urgency are expounded.

The notion of "holiness" is one of the most important biblical themes. All the grammatical terms for the idea—"holiness," "holy," "make holy" ("sanctify" or "hallow")—represent a fundamental reality in Israel's faith. "Holy" is one of the few predicate adjectives used of God. God is holy, and all holiness derives ultimately from him. "Holy" almost means "the divine," that is, that which belongs to the very being of God and to him alone. It is his difference or separateness from all else that exists. For Israel, it is the idea which gathers up all that is distinctive of the Covenant Lord in contrast with the heathen gods and the earth and its rebellious people. But holiness is not a static, unknowable quality of God. Israel's God acted in history, called a people, was at work reclaiming a world that was rightfully his. So his holiness breaks into the world and incorporates people, places, times, and things which he appropriates and chooses to use for his purpose. And at the climax of history his glory, the outward visible form of his holiness, will fill the earth. In this invasion, this movement of holiness into the profane, Israel had a special role. By God's election, he had sanctified these people and set them apart as peculiarly his. They were his beachhead in the invasion of the world by holiness. The entire force of this theology of holiness lies behind the exhortation to Israel: "You shall be holy; for I the LORD your God am holy." (On the relation of "holy" to "profane," "clean," and "unclean," see the introductory comment on Leviticus 11-16.)

On the Slaughter of Sacrificial Animals and the Use of Blood (17:1-16)

Verses 1-2 introduce four instructions for the priests and all Israel concerning the place where sacrifice is to be offered and how the blood of animals is to be handled. Each section begins with a phrase equivalent to "If any man of the house of Israel . . ." Each specifies the severest punishment for violation of its prohibition: the guilty shall be cut off from among the people, that is, excommunicated. (On the technical terms of sacrifice used here, see the comment on Leviticus 1-7.)

Verses 3-7 specify that whenever a man kills an animal quali-

fied for sacrifice (ox, lamb, goat) it must be taken to the priest
at the Tabernacle and slaughtered as a sacrifice of peace offering.
In this way slaughter of animals for food was reserved as a ritual
for the Temple, while the meat was returned to the man who
brought it (see Lev. 7:11-18). It appears that from early times
killing animals for food had been a ritual, usually performed at a
local sanctuary or high place. When these were destroyed and
worship was centered in the Jerusalem Temple by Josiah, the Deuteronomic law allowed the killing of animals for food at home
(Deut. 12:15-16). In Leviticus even that permission is withdrawn as further insurance that no ritual involving animal slaughter could possibly become a pagan ceremony. Verse 7 suggests
that sacrifices to "satyrs" (demons who were thought to take the
form of goats) were being offered by some people. The central-
ization motif of this section and the next is part of the unending
effort to consecrate all ritual purely and properly to the Lord.

Verses 8-9 require that burnt offerings and sacrifices (the latter
term probably includes here all other animal offerings) be brought
to the Tabernacle (Temple) as a sacrifice to the Lord. Sacrifice is
to be performed nowhere else and to no one else.

Verses 10-12 prohibit any Israelite or sojourner from eating
any blood, which includes meat with the blood in it (19:26). The
utter seriousness of this offense is emphasized in the tone of its
punishment: the Lord himself will set his face against a man who
eats blood and will cut him off from the people. The prohibition
of eating blood because it bears life in it begins with the era after
the Flood and so applies to all mankind as an ordinance of God
(Gen. 9:4); the law against it is repeated frequently (for example, Lev. 3:17; 7:26; Deut. 12:16). Appended to the prohibition here is the crucial interpretation of the significance of
blood in Israel's worship. It is the blood which is the instrument
of atonement (see Lev. 4). Blood is chosen because it is the bearer
of life (the personal vitality which animates a being as acting,
thinking, willing, feeling). When the blood of a sacrifice is offered, it involves and incorporates in its life the life of the worshiper, and it atones for his life (the same word in Hebrew is
behind the English "souls" and "life"). The ultimate reason for
the importance of blood, however, is the ordinance of God; he
establishes it for the purpose of atonement. And the phrase, "I
have given it ... upon the altar," means not only that God has
established the ordinance, but also that God is the actor in the

work of atonement. The priest represents God; man does not
atone for his own sin. In accord with this interpretation, the New
Testament says that "without the shedding of blood there is no
forgiveness of sins" (Heb. 9:22). The purpose of this ordinance
is realized in the death of Christ, through whose blood God
atones for our sins—his life for our lives—and we receive this
redemption by faith (Rom. 3:25; Eph. 1:7; Heb. 9; I John 1:7).

Verses 13-16 deal also with the prohibition of eating blood,
here in the case of animals taken in hunting or found dead or
crippled.

On Sexual Purity (18:1-30)

Throughout Israel's religious history, she had a faith about the
meaning and use of sex which was incomparably higher than the
views of surrounding peoples, and indeed superior to most contemporary cultures. Israel regarded sex as the creation of God for
the union of husband and wife and the bearing of children. It is
God's blessing upon man and woman, a way of love and fruitful-
ness. As the gift of God it was under his authority and regulated
by his commandments. The law consistently prohibits the use of
sex in worship or the promiscuous reign of desire which disturbs
the order of families.

The law (vss. 6-23) is set within an introduction (vss. 1-5)
and conclusion (vss. 24-30), both cast in the form of exhortation; this arrangement may indicate that the chapter was originally used for reading by the priest at a service of worship. The
exhortation identifies the prohibited sexual acts as things practiced by Egypt and Canaan; they belong to pagan ways and not
to the life of God's people. These defiling customs were an
abomination to the Lord, and were one of the reasons why the
Canaanites were cast out of their land.

The larger part of the law (vss. 6-18) forbids sexual relations
between a man and woman kin to each other in any way; the expression used here for the sexual act is "to uncover nakedness."
Verse 6 is the basic law, and verses 7-18 define in detail the ex-
tent of the kinship pattern covered by the law.

In verses 19-23 there are four laws dealing with intercourse
during the menstrual period, adultery, homosexuality, and sexual
use of animals. The law on sacrifice to Molech (vs. 21) may appear here because the worship of pagan gods was often described
as a sexual irregularity (on Molech, see comment on 20:1-27).

On Living the Holy Life (19:1-37)

This collection of some thirty laws covers what we would call both ritual and moral matters, although for Israel life was not separated into such independent spheres. Worship and work were united in one total movement of living which was to be sanctified and conformed to the nature and will of God. The introduction (vss. 1-2) and conclusion (vss. 36b-37) state the theological motif on which the laws are based: the Lord is Israel's God because he redeemed them from Egypt; therefore his holiness must define their life. Within the chapter the sentence "I am the LORD" (or "I am the LORD your God") is constantly repeated as a refrain to punctuate the entire series with this motif.

The collector (or collectors) of H assembled here a variety of laws which had been long current in Israel; counterparts of many of them are to be found in the Decalogue, the Book of the Covenant, and the Deuteronomic Code. The chapter seems to be an illustration of the way in which the Lord's will defines all the spheres of life: the cult, home, agriculture, the court, business, personal relations to other people. Within the collection there appear little codes or series of laws dealing with some one subject. This demonstrates that Israel had not only broad formulations of the law like the Decalogue, covering in summary fashion the whole of God's will, but also other "tables" of law to instruct the people about particular areas of existence. So many matters are dealt with in the chapter that the comment can hardly be more than a catalogue of its contents.

Verses 3-4 are laws similar to three in the Decalogue on reverence for parents, Sabbath-keeping, and the prohibition of idols.

Verses 5-8 regulate the eating of the sacrifice of peace offerings (see Lev. 7:15-18).

Verses 9-10 form a little law on harvesting, requiring that something be left in field and vineyard as a portion for the poor and the sojourner (see Deut. 24:19-22).

Verses 11-18 contain a series on community or social morality. They require honesty, truthfulness, and justice in dealing with other men. The typical concern for the claims of one's brother and neighbor (fellow Israelite and sojourner) appear in all, especially in the prohibition of hatred, vengeance, and grudges in Israel. The prohibition is positively stated in verse 18: "You shall love your neighbor as yourself."

This single sentence discloses in a crucial way the intention and basis of God's instruction for Israel. It transcends the legal idiom because it is stated positively and summons Israel to a way of love. It leaves off setting limits on man's lust for power and egoistic self-centeredness to prevent him from violating the life of others around him. It calls for a way of life that needs no checks because it is a kind of living which expresses the way of God, the way of love. Here, from within the Old Testament, a theme emerges to reach out to the Apostle Paul and his witness to the freedom of obedience. Paul unites the negative and positive in the admonition: "You were called to freedom, brethren; only do not use your freedom as an opportunity for the flesh, but through love be servants of one another. For the whole law is fulfilled in one word, 'You shall love your neighbor as yourself' " (Gal. 5:13-14). Here a way of life is portrayed which needs no negatives; "against such there is no law" (Gal. 5:23). Along with Deuteronomy 6:4-5, Leviticus 19:18 is quoted by Jesus as the interpretation of the whole will of God (Mark 12:28-31). Love of God and love of neighbor form the central way; the negatives of the Law are guideposts set from time to time to check the failures in our obedience. The negatives are never to be seen alone or apart from a relation to this center. They are not self-sufficient. If the believer obeys only the negatives he falls into the legalism of a law-religion. The negatives are there for the sake of the positive of love, without which they are incomplete.

In the story of the Good Samaritan, Jesus broadens the meaning of "neighbor" to cover every man near us in need.

Verses 19, 23-31 deal with ritual matters. Reverence for the created order of nature is required, pagan cultic practices are forbidden, and the produce of the land is regarded as sanctified to the Lord.

Verses 20-22 apply to the violation of the rights of a female slave.

Verses 32-36a are a miscellaneous series on conduct toward older people and sojourners, and on conduct in business.

On Spiritual and Physical Unchastity (20:1-27)

The various laws in this chapter are held together by the opening formula (vss. 1-2a) and a concluding exhortation (vss. 22-26). The longest section (vss. 10-21) contains laws dealing with sexual irregularities; the opening section (vss. 2b-5) prohibits in-

fant sacrifice to the god Molech. Two laws (vss. 6, 27) are concerned with mediums and wizards, and one (vs. 9) with the punishment for cursing parents. The reasons for grouping all these
together may be: (1) that all the laws deal with extremely serious
offenses which have as punishment that the offender either "be
put to death" or "be cut off from among their people"; (2) that
the worship of other gods was often called "playing the harlot"
(vss. 5-6), and so religious as well as sexual aberrations were
thought of in Israel as infidelity. Verse 9 on cursing parents fits
(1) but not (2).

"Molech" is a nickname for the god of the Ammonites, pronounced in Hebrew so that it is reminiscent of the word for
"shame." The name appears elsewhere as "Milcom" or "Moloch"
or "Malcarth." The specific prohibition of the sacrifice of children
to Molech by fire (see also 18:21) grew out of actual cases when
Israelites, even the king, fell into this horrible pagan practice (see
I Kings 11:5, 7; II Kings 21:6; II Chron. 28:3; Ezek. 23:37).

Mediums and wizards were diviners who gained information
for people by consulting the spirits of the dead. This kind of divination was common in the pagan religions; it was forbidden to
Israel not only for that reason, but also because it involved contact with the forbidden unclean realm of the dead.

The laws concerning sexual life are similar to those in 18:6-
23, except that here penalties are stated.

On the Sanctity of Israel's Worship (21:1—22:33)

These two chapters contain five sections which deal with the
preservation of the holiness of priests and sacrifices, and the condition of animals which may be offered to the Lord. The sections
are introduced by the formula "And the LORD said to Moses,"
and are addressed to the priests and, in one case (22:17), to the
people as well. The concluding exhortation (22:31-33) states the
theological concern of the whole. The people whom God has
set apart as his own (sanctified) shall hallow his holy name. Their
worship shall be in such awe and reverence as to honor him in every detail. In this matter the priests bear a special responsibility
because they handle the holy things of the sanctuary and offer
the sacrifices (21:6).

The particular provisions of these sections deal primarily with
problems of ritual uncleanness and the physical qualifications of
men and of the animals used in sacrifice. If Israel regarded this

meticulous care about physical matters as the only problem of approach to God, then the cult would be crassly external and irrelevantly legalistic. But the real intention of controlling the ritual and physical condition of people and animals in the cult was to honor with total reverence the holiness of God. Even the physical must display this holiness. This was Israel's way of act-ing out in her worship the petition, "Hallowed be thy name."

The first section, 21:1-15, is concerned with maintaining the sanctity of the priests (vss. 1-9) and the high priest (vss. 10-15). Their holiness comes by a consecrating act of God (vss. 8, 15) and must be rigidly respected. They are to observe the laws of clean and unclean (see Lev. 11-15), avoid marking their bodies or beards after the fashion of pagans, and marry only virgins from among their own people. The laws controlling the domestic life of the priests have a parallel in Paul's list of qualifications for bishops and deacons (I Tim. 3:1-13).

The next section, 21:16-23, forbids any member of the Aaronic family from acting as a priest if he has any of the physical in-firmities listed. The priest who draws near to God must be with-out blemish, a requirement which the author of Hebrews says that Christ met in a total way (Heb. 7:26).

Regulations regarding the use of "the holy things" appear in 22:1-16. These "holy things" are the part of an offering reserved for the priests as their portion (Lev. 1-7). Only those who are ritually clean and belong to the priest's household can eat conse-crated food.

The next section, 22:17-25, specifies that animals brought as an offering to the Lord must be without blemish in order to be acceptable. The perfectness of the offering was a testimony to the sincerity and integrity of him who brought it. The use of blind, lame, and sick animals was roundly condemned by Malachi as a cheating evasion of the demands of God's honor (Mal. 1:6-14).

In 22:26-30 two laws are added on the acceptability of animals for sacrifice and two on eating a thank offering.

On Israel's Holy Year (23:1-44)

This list enumerates in order the festivals and special days which made up the religious calendar of Israel. These were the occasions which marked a year's course and gave to time itself a rhythm of devotion, thanksgiving, and praise. By observing them, Israel testified to the saving history by which the Lord had given her existence as his people, recognized that her very physical life was dependent on him, and consecrated all of her common life to God. The year itself became a witness to him who was Lord of time and history. This particular chapter is concerned with the dates of the festivals and convocations and with the character of the celebrations which belonged to them. In Numbers 28-29 the regulations for the sacrifices for each feast and convocation are given.

In this calendar, months are identified only by their number, a regular practice of the P tradition. Months are numbered beginning with late March-early April, according to the Babylonian system which Israel adopted in the exilic period. Earlier Israel had used the Canaanite calendar, which began in autumn. Leviticus 23 describes the religious year of postexilic Israel and represents the latest phase of the history of the religious calendar in the Old Testament. Strictly speaking, there were only three "appointed feasts": Unleavened Bread, Weeks, and Booths. These were the great pilgrim festivals, the three times in the year when all Israel had to appear "before the LORD" at the central shrine where the Ark was kept. They are required in the very earliest laws of Israel (see Exod. 23:14-17; 34:18-23; and for the Deuteronomic version, Deut. 16:1-17). Other fixed times for holy convocations are added here to produce a complete religious calendar, and materials are drawn from at least two distinct sources (H along with P). Notice that there are two introductions (vss. 1-2 and vs. 4) which allow for an incorporation of the Sabbath in the list, and also an appendix (vss. 39-43) after the summary conclusion (vss. 37-38).

The weekly Sabbath (vs. 3) had become in postexilic times the holy day of Israel above all else. Its basic ordinance is given in the first creation story (Gen. 2:1-3) and in the fourth commandment (Exod. 20:8-11). By freedom from labor on one day, Israel consecrated each week and its labor, remembered that the earth was the Lord's, and testified through the very arrangement of time into weeks of seven days that creation was complete and good through the perfect work of God.

Verses 5-14 deal with the complex of celebrations which began in the first month of the year in the spring. Passover, which is no more than dated here, fell on the evening of the fourteenth day (vs. 5). It is the oldest feast of Israel and was probably observed in an earlier form by Israel's ancestors before they came to Canaan. It was recast as an Exodus ritual to celebrate the Lord's "passing over" Israel on the evening before their deliverance from Egypt. Its institution appears in Exodus 12:1-13, 21-27. The Feast of Unleavened Bread follows Passover immediately, beginning on the fifteenth and lasting for seven days. It was originally a festival of the Canaanites, whose religion was oriented to the agricultural year; its purpose was the celebration of the beginning of the barley harvest. Israel adopted the festival so that the devotion of the harvest would be to the Lord, and not to Canaanite gods. The festival was given a peculiarly Israelite nature by the insertion of a motif from the Exodus; the Israelites ate unleavened bread to remember their haste in preparing to leave Egypt (see the texts of institution in Exod. 12:15-20; 13:3-10). Unleavened bread was probably employed in the original agricultural festival to insure the fact that none of the old dough from the previous year's harvest would be used to provide yeast for the bread of the new harvest.

The ritual of First Fruits described in verses 9-14 appears nowhere else in the Pentateuch, but it seems to belong in this calendar to the celebration of Unleavened Bread. The dedication of the first grain of the harvest to the Lord was certainly a very ancient practice in Israel. In Deuteronomy 26:1-11 there is a description of how the Israelite brought the first of his harvest for presentation to the Lord of the shrine; he presents the offering and then recites a confession to show that the land which he farms is a gift of the Lord through the saving history, thus uniting the historical and agricultural themes of his faith. Here a sheaf of the first harvest is brought to the priest (Lev. 23:11), who waves it to and fro before the place of God's presence to show that the harvest is dedicated in dependence and thanksgiving to him who gives it. Then certain offerings are made to complete the ritual.

The final festival of the early year is described in verses 15-22. Its usual name, not given here, is the Feast of Weeks (Deut. 16:10), so called because its date was determined by reckoning seven weeks plus one day from the Sabbath of First Fruits (note the relation of "the sabbath" in verse 15 to "the sabbath" in verse 11). The interval of fifty days led to the later name of Pentecost, used in the New Testament. The seven weeks was the approximate duration of the harvest, and at its conclusion a holy convocation was called for the presentation of the bread of the harvest and for bringing cereal, burnt, and sin offerings. In later Judaism the feast was used to celebrate the giving of the Law at Sinai, because of the similarity of the seven weeks to the interval between the Exodus and the arrival of Israel at the Mount of God.

In the fall, the beginning of the old Israelite year was marked by a ceremony of the blowing of trumpets, and a day of solemn rest was observed (vss. 23-25). What had been a celebration of vast importance in early pre-exilic Israel was diminished by the end of the monarchy, whose kings played a significant role in the New Year's celebration, and by the change in the calendar from a beginning in the fall to a beginning in the spring.

The Day of Atonement (vss. 26-32) was held on the tenth day of the seventh month. (On this holy convocation, see the comment on Leviticus 16.)

The Feast of Booths (vss. 33-36, 39-43) was held for a week, beginning on the fifteenth of the seventh month. It was primarily a vintage festival which marked the conclusion of the entire harvest, when all the produce of the land had been gathered. In this annual "thanksgiving" the Israelites assembled to rejoice (celebrate in festive merriment), holding processions in which they carried fruit and waved the branches of trees. The feast was called "booths" because of the custom of living in huts or shelters made from the branches of trees. Israel saw in this custom a dramatic reliving of the Exodus time when the people lived in temporary shelters in the wilderness. According to Deuteronomy 31:9-13, every seven years the Law was to be read during this feast; in the time of the monarchy the Feast of Booths may have included a ceremony in which the Covenant between Israel and the Lord was renewed.

Throughout Israel's religious calendar two themes are joined: the rhythm of the agricultural year and the crucial moments in the salvation history accomplished by the Lord in the Exodus, at Sinai, and in the wilderness. In Israel's faith the relationship of the two was not forced. The land on which Israel dwelt and whose fertility she enjoyed was an inheritance given Israel by God, according to the promise to the fathers and as the climax of the salvation history. Land and history were inseparably joined in Israel's faith. In contrast to the other religions around her, Israel knew God through unique events in her history and not in the yearly phases of nature. Nature was subjected to history and was interpreted by the salvation history, so that every passing year pointed beyond itself to the changeless God whose Person was above nature, and whose purpose spanned all the years and set them in one total movement toward the coming of his Kingdom.

On the Lamp and the Bread of the Presence (24:1-9)

Although chapter 24 as a whole is introduced by the formula in verse 1, it is divided by reason of subject and source. Verses 1-9 are a part of P and depend on instructions concerning the preparation of the Tabernacle in Exodus. The instruction to keep the lamp alight from evening to morning before the Holy of Holies is similar to Exodus 27:20-21. The lampstand is described in Exodus 25:31-40. The twelve cakes of bread represented the twelve tribes of Israel and were to be placed on the table in the Tabernacle (see Exod. 25:23-30). These cakes are called elsewhere "the bread of the Presence" (showbread), and were a form of offering to the Lord.

The light and the bread were Israel's way in ritual to serve the indwelling Presence in the sanctuary. They knew he did not need the light or eat the bread, but having them was a human way of recognizing and testifying that by his grace God was in their midst.

On Blasphemy Against the Name of God (24:10-23)

The purpose of this story about the man who blasphemed the name of God is to show how the death penalty for this sin originated in Mosaic times at the command of God. The story belongs to the P material; in form and function it is similar to the one about the punishment of the man found working on the Sabbath (Num. 15:32-36). Set within the story are a series of laws (vss. 15-22), placed here because the first one (vss. 15-16) deals with blasphemy against the name of the Lord. This little series bears the marks of having belonged originally to H.

In very late times Israel, out of reverence, would not even pronounce the proper name of her God, so holy was the name considered to be. But this story is hardly based on that practice. The sin seems rather to have been a belittling defamation of Israel's God, a rejection of reverence for his authority and his right over Israel. The "name" of God was that by which God made himself known to Israel (Exod. 3:13-15); to pronounce the "name" was a way of confessing faith and calling upon God. Blaspheming the name was by the same token a rejection of God. Such a crime put the whole people in danger of God's wrath, and they were made responsible for purging the sinner from their midst. In regard to the punishment we must remember that in Israel the civil and religious communities were identical. Whether the punishment seems too severe depends on the seriousness with which one regards the rejection of God. The Church does not mete out punishment, but it does pray and live for the hallowing of God's name; nor could it long exist if God's name were blasphemed in its fellowship.

The little code in verses 15-22 contains laws based on the *lex talionis*, the law of retaliation—life for life, eye for eye, tooth for tooth. This strict and harsh requirement belongs to the same law which requires that a man love his neighbor as himself (19:17-18). The law of retaliation was a community rather than a personal matter. The social group had to hold each member responsible for the life and health and property of others. How this is to be done is a continuing great problem; that it must be done the Church must always insist. Since, in our society, Church and state are separate, the Church must raise its voice in the society to call upon the state to hold men responsible for and to one another.

On the Sabbath Year and the Year of Jubilee (25:1-55)

Besides the annual feasts and holy convocations listed in chapter 23, the law of holiness provides for two which are reckoned in a calendar of years: the Sabbath Year which, like the weekly Sabbath observed every seven days, came every seventh year; and the Year of Jubilee, the fiftieth year, after seven "weeks" of years. The basic observance of the Sabbath Year was a complete rest for the land. No crops were to be sown, nor was a full harvest to be made. Israel was to live off what grew of its own accord in the fields and vineyards. The Year of Jubilee provided for a general overhaul of economic and social life to restore persons and property to their rightful conditions. Land was to be returned to its original owners, slaves were to be set free. It was meant to be a kind of new beginning, a point in time when all who had failed to maintain their place in society were given a chance to start over.

In this long chapter only verses 1-7 and verses 18-22 deal with the Sabbath Year. Verses 8-12 describe the basic institution of the Year of Jubilee. The remainder of the chapter is concerned with procedures for buying and selling property and dealing with

slaves in the light of the institution. Interspersed are laws on own-
ership of land and debts between Israelites, similar to some appearing elsewhere in the Old Testament. The legislation on the
Sabbath Year and these individual laws seem to come from H;
the bulk of the remainder has been added by P.

The observance of a Sabbath Year goes back into Israel's early
history, for a law requiring it appears in the Book of the Covenant (Exod. 23:10-11). We do not know how the institution was
observed, whether for individual pieces of land in turn (as is probable), or as a general rest for all the land. The latter is to be
the practice according to Leviticus 25. The very land is to observe the Sabbath, and in its rest from cultivation is to manifest
its createdness and to confess the nature of the earth and its produce as the work of God.

The name "Jubilee" is a Greek form of the Hebrew word for
"trumpet"; the fiftieth year was to open with the blowing of the
trumpet throughout the land (vs. 9). The Year of Jubilee is not
mentioned elsewhere in the Old Testament, and we have no historical proof that it was ever observed. But the intention of the
ordinance is clear enough. Israel was to observe a special Sabbath
Year when every man returned to his property and his family.
Liberty was proclaimed throughout the land to all its inhabitants
(vs. 10). The problem at which the year was directed was one
with which Israel wrestled from the time when she settled in
Canaan. In the old faith of Israel every man was to be free and to
have his inviolable place as a member of the people. And the
land was a gift from God, distributed to the families of the tribes
as a sacrament of their place in the promise of God. But when
Israel's economy developed in the direction of business practices
of the surrounding peoples, land was lost and Israelites fell into
bondslavery through debts. Prophets and Covenant law struggled
against this development. The law against taking interest from a
brother Israelite (vss. 35-37) is a part of this effort to exclude
profiteering on the weaker members of society. Another social
device to maintain every man's liberty and each family's property
was the institution of the "redeemer" (see vss. 25-28 and 47-54)
—the name for the next of kin whose right and responsibility it
was to buy back ("redeem") his kinsman from slavery or his
kinsman's property from another. In the Year of Jubilee, Israel
sought to provide in her very liturgical calendar a way and time
for putting the social order right. Whether it was ever observed

or not, the requirement stands as a witness that God wills liberty and integrity for every man in the actualities of his social existence.

The Final Exhortation (26:1-46)

The law of holiness reaches its conclusion in a great exhortation which argues with resounding eloquence how crucial it is for Israel to obey the commandments of the Lord. Life in the Promised Land is at stake. If the people obey, the land will be abundantly fruitful and the nation will be strong against its enemies, will have peace, and will enjoy the presence of God. But if they refuse and scorn God's commandments, the hammer blows of his wrath will fall upon them, until they either repent or lose every visible reality of their existence as the People of the Lord. This basic argument appears in hortatory conclusions at the end of Israel's other two great law codes (for the Book of the Covenant, Exod. 23:20-33; and for the Deuteronomic law, Deut. 28), but is delivered here in the characteristic style of H. In the Old Testament, law is the will of the Lord for the life of the people whom he has delivered and made his own; this exhortation proclaims the meaning and consequence of that fact.

The exhortation is introduced (vss. 1-2) by a summary statement of laws already given; they cover the first four commandments of the Decalogue and seem to be placed here as an epitome of the heart of the Law. The exhortation proper begins with a review of the blessings which follow obedience (vss. 3-13). Then comes a longer section describing the punishments which God will send for disobedience, arranged in ascending order and reaching a climax in the loss of the land and exile (vss. 14-39). Then there is a concluding section which describes how the Lord will remember the people if they repent (vss. 40-45). Verse 46 is the conclusion for the entire law of holiness.

This message from God at the end of this body of the Law places it in the only relationship in which it is to be understood and interpreted. This law is the will of "the LORD your God, who brought you forth out of the land of Egypt, that you should not be their slaves; and I have broken the bars of your yoke and made you walk erect" (vs. 13). God's claim upon Israel is based on his deliverance. His law is not a way for them to qualify to become the People of God; it is the way the people of Israel are to live because they have been set free to be the People of God.

They are set free from the tyrants of history to serve the true Lord of history whose service is true life.

Therefore the Covenant is the theme of the whole exhortation (vss. 9, 12, 15, 42, 44-45). The blessings which accompany obedience are the confirmation of the Covenant. But if Israel rejects the will of the Lord as her way of life, then she is guilty of breaking the Covenant and must suffer the penalties due her. Yet, the door of hope is always open from God's side. If the people confess their iniquity and repent, then the Lord will "remember the covenant with their forefathers." Even in their sin and rebellion he will not cease to be "their God."

The tenor of the entire exhortation is very much that of the prophets in their preaching to Israel. The history of Israel turns on a moral pivot; what happens has an ethical meaning and Israel is responsible under God for her own history.

The Commutation of Vows and Tithes (Lev. 27:1-34)

When an Israelite prayed for help or blessing he could accompany the prayer with a "vow" by which he promised to give something to the priest for the Lord when the prayer was answered. That which was promised became "dedicated" or "consecrated"; it was no longer at the disposal of its owner. The first part of this chapter sets forth an arrangement by which the man who made the vow could substitute a money payment estimated by the priest, instead of the dedicated thing. A vow could dedicate persons (vss. 2-8), animals (vss. 9-13), houses (vss. 14-15), and part of one's land (vss. 16-25). The first-born of animals (vss. 26-27) were already sacred according to the law and could not be dedicated in a vow. "Devoted" persons or things (that is, put under the ban for destruction or execution) could not be redeemed as vows could (vss. 28-29). This practice of substituting money for a vow according to very precise and detailed regulation was a rather late development. It may have originated with the much earlier custom of redeeming the dedicated first-born child (Exod. 13:11-16) and spread to all classes of dedicated things.

The principle of commutation is here applied also to the tithe, the tenth of his produce and income owed by every Israelite to the Lord (vss. 30-33). Money might be substituted for produce by the addition of one-fifth of its value.

The material all comes from the latest strata of the P source; it presupposes the institution of the Year of Jubilee. The chapter is probably placed here because of the reference in chapter 25 to the Jubilee and the custom of redeeming. Verse 34 is a subscription for all the legal material associated with Sinai.

The Preparation for Pilgrimage (Num. 1:1—10:10)

The narrative telling about Israel's camp at Sinai runs on into Numbers, ending in the tenth chapter when the cloud moves from the Tabernacle and precedes the tribes into the wilderness of Paran (10:11-28). Because they are set at Sinai, the events and laws of this material have the same permanent validity for the foundation of Israel's life under the Lord as the matters previously dealt with in Exodus and Leviticus.

What gives this section its distinctiveness is the fact that its material is concerned with Israel's preparation for the march through the wilderness under God's guidance. Up to this point Israel's stance had been that of a waiting, listening community; the time had been filled with the massive communication between God and people through Moses concerning the formation of the tribes as the People of the Lord. The listening does not break off, for as before, almost every section is introduced by the constant formula of revelation, "And the LORD said to Moses . . ." But now a response and movement begins to stir in the vast camp. A shifting, regrouping, organizing effort takes place, the goal of which is to achieve that order and readiness which belong to the People of the Lord as they move through the wilderness toward the Promised Land.

After the first census (ch. 1), whose purpose is to arrange the people for the march, the stir continues (ch. 2). The organization of the Levites (chs. 3, 4, and 8) provides for the care of the Tabernacle on the march. The offerings of the leaders (ch. 7) muster the resources of the tribes to serve the Tabernacle in its transport. The sanctity of the camp is required (ch. 5). Israel's second Passover is celebrated (ch. 9), to mark the passage of a year since the deliverance from Egypt. The lamps are lighted in the Tabernacle (8:1-4), guidance for the trackless wilderness is provided (9:15-23), trumpets to signal the host are made (10: 1-10). The whole panorama combines the characteristics of an army preparing for a campaign and a Church in the final stages

of organization. And this is precisely the point. Israel is portrayed as the Church militant, preparing for the history in which
God establishes his lordship over his world. Sinai is not a shrine
for a monastic community which has withdrawn from the world
for mystic communion. It is the source of a spring which flows
out into the world, gathering momentum and force until it is a
mighty torrent, whose waters shall one day revive a new Eden in
a wilderness world that has made the old Eden wither. Sinai is not
just a place; it is also a time at which God sets his own direction
within history, and Israel's story becomes a movement toward a
destiny that transcends place and time because it is the fulfillment
of the promise, "In you all the families of the earth shall be
blessed" (Gen. 12:3, margin).

The First Census (1:1-54)

The initial step in preparing to break the year-old camp at
Sinai was a census, conducted at the command of God. In each
tribe the men who were twenty and older were numbered to determine all in Israel who were able to go to war. Both in purpose and
procedure the census was military; it was a way to organize and
prepare the men of Israel for the holy war which lay ahead, for
the struggle in which they would serve the Holy God in this conquest of the earth over which he is rightfully Lord. The census
was carried out by tribe, by family, and by fathers' house; it reflects in its procedure the Priestly tradition concerning the ideal
symmetrical structure of Israel, that is, the twelve-tribe federation,
organized around the central Tabernacle of God's presence. The
pilgrimage to the Promised Land was God's own campaign, and
he levies the troops for its service.

The chapter tells first of God's command to Moses to take the
census, and of the selection of a leader from each tribe to assist,
obviously as the commanding officer of that tribe's forces (vss.
1-16). Then Moses and Aaron take the census, beginning with
Reuben and ending with Naphtali (vss. 17-46). The total for all
twelve tribes came to 603,550 men. The Levites were not numbered in this census (vss. 47-54), because they were reserved for
the service of the Tabernacle; in the pilgrimage the care of the
Tabernacle was their vocation. By counting Ephraim and Manasseh, the sons of Joseph, as two tribes, the number twelve was
maintained in the military census.

The large totals have long been a subject of controversy. If there were more than 600,000 men over twenty years old, there would have been more than two million Israelites in the wilderness, counting women and children. The figure seems out of the question for a group living in the barren territory of the wilderness. Moreover, it does not agree with other biblical figures concerning the size of Israel during the later period of the Judges (for example, Judges 5:8; 18:11). Many have concluded that the list is artificial, an arbitrary construction of Priestly tradition.

Recent study of the text in relation to lists for military levy coming from other neighboring peoples during this period indicates that the Priestly writer may have had before him an old document, dating from the early days of the monarchy. The Hebrew word in this chapter which is translated "thousand" seems to have been the designation of a military unit in early Israel, as well as a specific number. The list gives, not one arithmetical total, but the number of units and then the total number of men in these units. The levy for Reuben (vs. 21) then would be 46 units with a total of 500 men. Calculating in this way, a total for all Israel would be 5,550 men in 598 units. This pattern of military organization fits in well with what is known from the period of early Israel's history. Because the technical meaning of the Hebrew word had fallen out of use, the framers of the Priestly tradition understood it in its usual meaning of "thousand."

The Order of Israel for Camp and March (2:1-34)

The people who were mustered for military service in the census are now organized for their life in the wilderness. God gives Moses and Aaron a pattern for arranging the tribes when they camp and as they march. The Tent of Meeting is always to be in the center. In the camp, the tribes are to surround it, with three on each of its sides. One principal tribe is to plant its standard on its appointed side, with two others on either hand. Judah was given the place of honor on the east, facing the door of the Tent; Issachar and Zebulon camped with Judah. On the south was Reuben with Simeon and Gad, on the west Ephraim with Manasseh and Benjamin, and on the north Dan with Asher and Naphtali. When the tribes broke camp, they were to set out in like order: Judah's group first, then Reuben's, Ephraim's, and Dan's. The Tent of Meeting was to be carried by the Levites in the center of the column of march, between Reuben and Ephraim. The arrangement of the Levites is described in chapter 3.

There is no certainty as to what actual practice of camp organization or what tradition about Israel's wilderness life is here used by the Priestly writer. But the central idea of faith which the pattern manifests is clear. Israel, as the Covenant People of God, formed a collection of tribes and clans whose unity and organizing focus was the presence of God in their midst. All of their national life was to be organized around the dominant reality that the Lord was with them.

The Institution of the Levites (3:1—4:49)

As one more step in completing arrangements for the service of the Tabernacle, God commands that the entire tribe of Levi be numbered, organized, and assigned a place around the Tabernacle in the camp and be given duties in moving it on the march. In the first census, Levi was passed over because of the special vocation the tribe was to have in Israel (1:47-54). When the other tribes were arranged around the Tabernacle (ch. 2), the arrangement of the Levites was not settled (2:17). Now both matters are cared for.

In the Priestly narrative up to this point, the tribe of Levi had been simply one of the twelve tribes. They were indeed distinguished by the fact that Moses and Aaron were of their number (see Exod. 6:14-25), but Aaron's elevation to the priesthood had not affected their status. In the incident of the golden calf (an older story) the tribe had gotten special honor because of its fervent zeal for the cause of the Lord (Exod. 32:25-29). Here, before Israel leaves Sinai, they are singled out to be the tribe of the Lord in a special way. They become a special clergy who assist the priests in their work, and who serve all Israel by doing the tasks which the maintenance and transport of the Tabernacle involved. This one tribe is set aside to undertake the responsibility of all Israel by a ministry to the Meeting Place where the Lord confronts his people. They were called to be true servants and to minister to priests and people for the sake of the worship of God.

The account begins with the genealogy of Moses and Aaron (3:1-4). The genealogy is introduced by the formula "These are the generations of . . . ," a device by which the Priestly narrator marks the beginning of a significant section of his history and shows how crucial the institution of the Levites as a sacred tribe is for the holy history of God's people. In fact, only the descendants of Aaron are given, so as to identify the particular Levitical family who are the priests with whom the Levites as a whole are to work. The story of Nadab and Abihu appears in Leviticus 10.

The instituting command of the Lord, founding the sacred Levitical order, summarizes its status and duties (3:5-10). The Levites were to be brought near; that is, they were to be introduced into the sacred precincts of the Tabernacle, where only the priests were eligible to go. There they were to assist Aaron and his sons and be responsible for the structure and furnishings of the Tabernacle, a work which could not be done by the rest of Israel because the approach of unqualified persons to the Holy Place brought the danger of death.

An interpretation of the sacral status of the Levites is given in 3:11-13, 40-51. According to the story of Israel's deliverance from Egypt, when the Lord slew the first-born of man and beast among the Egyptians, he consecrated the first-born of Israel to himself as a memorial of the deliverance (Exod. 13:1-2, 11-16). First-born animals were to be sacrificed to the Lord, but first-born sons were to be redeemed by the substitution of a payment of money (see also Exod. 22:29; 34:19-20; Num. 18:15-16). Now the Levites are taken by the Lord as the redemption of all the first-born males in Israel, and their very office becomes a perpetual sign of Israel's deliverance. The ministry of the Levites proclaims to Israel the fact that all belong to the Lord, because he has delivered them. In 3:40-51 a census is taken of all first-born males in Israel, and the Levites are substituted for them as their redemption, one for one. Because there were 273 unredeemed first-born remaining when the number of Levites were exhausted, the money payment of five shekels each was accepted for them. So the installation of the Levites became a vast ceremony of redemption; the people of Israel would always know that the Levites stood in their place.

In the rest of chapter 3 (vss. 14-39) and in chapter 4 the Levites are numbered, arranged around the Tabernacle, and assigned their special duties by division. Whereas the census and arrangement of the rest of Israel has proceeded by tribes, in Levi it is by the houses of the three fathers: Gershon, Kohath, and Merari, the sons of Levi. These three in turn are divided into clans: Gershon into Libni and Shimei, with Eliasaph as their chief and Ithamar the son of Aaron in charge; Kohath into Amram, Izhar, Hebron, and Uzziel, with Elizaphan as chief and Eleazar the son of Aaron in charge; Merari into Mahli and Mushi, with

Zuriel as chief and Ithamar the son of Aaron in charge. Eleazar, who is to be the successor to Aaron as chief priest, is placed over the entire organization.

The Levites were arranged in a square around the Tabernacle, as a rank of the camp within the outer square of the tribes. The Aaronite priests and Moses camped on the east, in the place of honor at the opening of the Tabernacle. The Gershonites were placed on the west, at its rear. Their responsibility was the fabric and skin coverings and hangings of the Tabernacle. The Kohathites, camping on the south side, were assigned the Ark and all the cultic paraphernalia. On the north were Merarites, who saw to the frames of the Tabernacle. So the arrangement and duties of the Levites provided a corps of lesser clergy to guard the Holy Tent from profanation by the secular tribes, to tend it on the march, and to assist the sons of Aaron in their religious duties.

Historically speaking, this picture of the Levites given in Numbers 3 and 4 is true for the time of the Second Temple, after the Jews had come back from their Babylonian exile. The theological purpose of the Priestly narrative here, as always, is to anchor the religious institution of the Second Temple in the Mosaic foundation of Israel's religion at Sinai. The portrayal of the Levites as a minor clergy, assisting but having no part in the priesthood, fits only the latest stage of the long development through which the Levites passed in Israel's history. Levi appears in Israel's earliest tradition as a secular tribe, but from the time of the foundation of Israel's Covenant religion, the Levites had acquired a special status as especially qualified to be priests. By the time of Josiah's reform in the seventh century, all priests were Levites. It was Josiah's destruction of all centers of worship in favor of the Jerusalem Temple which initiated their decline. Naturally, those Levites in Jerusalem among the priesthood of its Temple had the prerogative of circumstance. With privilege went power, until finally the descendants of Aaron in Jerusalem alone had priestly status, while the Levites were organized into rotating corps of assistants who came to serve their term. The Priestly narrative sees the past in terms of its own situation to remind the later Jews that their Temple must always be for them the Tabernacle established by the Lord at Sinai.

On the Sanctity of the Camp (5:1-4)

Now that Israel is organized into a camp arranged around the

Tabernacle presided over by the Aaronic priests and tended by
the Levites (Num. 1-4), God commands that all who would defile the camp by reason of their uncleanness be put outside its
limits. In the Priestly history "the camp" is not just a place; it is
the theological symbol of the holy Congregation, the Church of
the sanctified People of God. God dwells in its midst; the uncleanness of sin cannot be accommodated to his holy Presence.
Those whose uncleanness is diagnosed in the law of purification
(Lev. 11-15)—the lepers, those having a bodily discharge, and
those who have touched the dead—must be put outside the
sacred precincts. The law of purification provided for their
cleansing, but while they were unclean they could not share the
life of the People of God. This seems harsh and ungracious, and
even contradictory to the redemptive nature of God. But we
must not forget that in the New Testament also, the sanctity of
God's people is rigorously maintained; the Church is to be clean,
a testimony to the holiness of God (Rom 12:1-2; I Cor. 5:9-13;
6:18-20; II Cor. 7:1). The mercy of God in his Son does not
mean that God accepts the sin of the sinner. But Jesus goes outside the camp to sanctify those who are excluded. He heals the
leper (Mark 1:40-45), touches those who have an issue (Mark
5:25-34), and lays his hand upon the dead (Luke 8:49-56). In
him, God, having set up his colony of saints, goes outside (Heb.
13:12) to bring in all who will accept his help and be cleansed
by his sacrifice.

On Restitution and Sacrifice for Sin (5:5-10)

All who break faith with the Lord by wronging their fellows
are guilty, and their guilt must be dealt with by confession and
sacrifice to God and restitution given to the injured brother.
These verses are largely a repetition of Leviticus 6:1-7 (see the
comment there), but they add provision for making restitution
to a kinsman, if the injured brother is dead. The section is placed
here to reinforce the insistence of verses 1-4 that conditions and
conduct which contradict God's holiness are a problem which
the Church cannot evade.

Trial by Ordeal for an Accused Wife (5:11-31)

These verses describe in exact detail the procedures to be
followed for the ritual testing of a woman whose husband suspects
her of adultery. The husband would bring her to the priest at the

Tabernacle, along with an appropriate cereal offering. The priest would put the woman "before the LORD" and make her recite a curse upon herself, the effect of which would be felt if she were guilty. He would prepare a ritual drink made of holy water and dust from the Tabernacle floor (5:17), into which he would wash the ink with which the curse was written (5:23). The woman would drink the mixture, which if she were guilty would cause her to become grievously ill. If no lasting physical effects resulted, she was innocent.

This ceremony represents a use of ritual magic which is without counterpart elsewhere in the law of Israel. To us it seems like cruel and crass superstition. It is certainly part of the ceremony which is done away in Jesus Christ. But we ought, in interpreting its use in the Church of the Old Testament, to remember the conditions of the day. The ordeal was not, as were many used by other ancient peoples for testing guilt, physically dangerous. It would seriously threaten only the guilty, and it would have been no more psychically injurious than many public divorce trials today. Israel viewed adultery as a terrible sin. Where it was suspected, the issue had to be resolved or the marriage would be ruined. This ceremonial trial did settle the matter. The woman knew herself to be in the hands of a God who was utterly just and merciful, and so was better off than in the eyes of a husband made irrational through uncontrolled jealousy. One could suspect that some contemporary women might wish for such relief from unjustified suspicion.

The Law for a Nazirite (6:1-21)

"Nazirite" means one who is "consecrated to God" by his very manner of life. The Nazirite took a vow to separate himself to the Lord; and the purpose of his peculiar way of life was to enforce the undivided dedication of Israel to the Lord as the one God for them. There were three marks of his separated life: First, he was not to eat or drink anything which came from the grapevine; the grape represented the culture of Canaan and was associated with Canaanite pagan ritual in many ways. He was to have the enthusiasm of the Spirit and not be intoxicated with wine (Eph. 5:18). Second, his hair was to grow uncut, a symbol of opposition to the new, civilized ways of Canaan. He was to live in the vital spontaneity which was natural to the old wilderness existence. Third, he was to touch no dead body, lest its uncleanness destroy the holiness of his separation (see Num. 5:2-3). By his consecration a Nazirite reminded his fellows of their own dedication to the Lord who required of them a different and special life.

Nazirites appear throughout Israel's history. Samson (Judges 13-16) is the most famous. Samuel seems to have been consecrated as a Nazirite by Hannah (I Sam. 1:11, 28). Amos ranks the Nazirites along with the prophets as crucial for the faithfulness of the Covenant People (Amos 2:11-12). The law in Numbers 6 represents the latest stage in the history of the Nazirite. Here the vow could be made for a specified period rather than for life. Where a ritual to conclude the vow was requisite, the Nazirite had to turn to the priest, so the ritual for the time of separation is set forth in verses 13-20. (On the types of sacrifice required—the burnt offering, the sin offering, and the peace offering—see the comment on Leviticus 1-7.)

The Priestly Blessing (6:22-27)

From time immemorial, it had been part of the priest's office to bless the congregation of Israel in the name of the Lord. When the installation of Aaron was complete, his first act was to turn to the people and to bless them (Lev. 9:22); here in verses 24-26 is recorded the formula of blessing which he would have used. Verses 22-23 give this prerogative to the Aaronic priesthood, reflecting the situation of the postexilic Temple. In the time of the monarchy, the Levites pronounced the blessing (Deut. 10:8), and even the king could do it on occasion (II Sam. 6:18). The words of the blessing proper are very early; Psalm 67 gives us their counterpart in a hymn.

In the Old Testament, the name of the Lord is the spoken reality of his personal presence and power; his name, used in faith and reverence, invoked God's presence and power. The blessing which "put" the name of the Lord upon Israel is a poem composed of three lines, each with two parts. The first part of each line invokes God's personal act upon his people: "bless . . . make his face to shine . . . lift up his countenance upon" (literally, "face towards"). The last two are gestures of favor and help. The last part of each line states the reality or content of the blessing invoked. God is to keep Israel, that is, guard her against foes and misfortune. He is to be gracious, showing his favor in love and mercy in dealing with their weakness and fail-

ures. The "peace" which he is to give them means more than
the absence of hostilities; it is the total welfare and health—
indeed, the entire salvation which belongs to those whose corporate lives are in harmony with God.

The priest as representative of the people prays to God for
these blessings, and as God's anointed he bespeaks over the
people God's will to bless. Thus the priest keeps the Old Testament Church under the ancient sign of the promise of God to
Abraham; they are the people through whom God offers blessing
instead of curse to the world.

The Offerings of the Leaders (7:1-89)

When the Tabernacle had been erected and consecrated, the
leaders of the tribes of Israel on their own initiative brought gifts
to care for the transporting and the sacrificial ritual of the Tabernacle. Their spontaneous and generous stewardship was example
and exhortation to Israel in every age. The People of God ought
to provide for the place of worship and give to meet its needs.

This long description of the leaders' generosity is an outstanding illustration of the characteristics of the style of the Priestly
narrative. First, the twelve leaders brought six covered vehicles
in which to move the Tabernacle, with twelve oxen to draw
them (vss. 1-9). These were turned over to the Levites for their
use during the march. Then, day by day for twelve days, each
leader brought an offering of gold and silver vessels with material for sacrifice: fine flour and oil, incense, rams, oxen, lambs,
and goats (vss. 10-88). The entire procedure is related in exact
detail of order and quantity, with a final summary in which the
totals are given. The chapter reads more like the report of an
accountant than like a narrative.

Verse 89 concludes more than just this chapter. When Moses
went into the Tent of Meeting he heard the voice of the Lord
speaking to him. The voice came from above the Ark, from the
empty space framed by the outstretched wings of the cherubim.
This was the central purpose of the entire preparation of the
Tabernacle—that God might dwell in the midst of his people
and his voice be heard. When Moses hears the voice, all has been
brought to culmination in arranging for the divine Presence.

Lighting the Lamp in the Tabernacle (8:1-4)

The golden lampstand, whose making is described in Exodus

25:31-40, stood within the Holy Place of the Tabernacle, to the left as one entered. Now Aaron, at the command of God, lights the lamps on its seven branches. The lighting of the lamps is the final act of readying the Tabernacle and seems to be the ritual for the beginning of its use.

The Consecration of the Levites (8:5-26)

The Levites, who were numbered and organized for the service of the Tabernacle in the events described in chapters 3-4, were now cleansed and set aside for their work. The ceremony for their installation parallels that for the priests, but was not so intense (see Lev. 8). They washed and shaved their bodies and washed their clothes. The entire congregation having assembled, the other Israelites laid their hands on their heads in an act of committal to office, constituting them as their representatives. A burnt offering and a sin offering were made for them. Thus the Levites, by this ritual, became the Lord's special tribe. They were the "wave offering" from Israel to the Lord, and the substitute for the consecration of the first-born in Israel. (On this interpretation of the service of the Levites, see the comment on Numbers 3-4.)

The Second Passover (9:1-14)

Israel had celebrated the first Passover in Egypt on the eve of deliverance from bondage (Exod. 12), and this great sacrament of salvation had become the time of all times. Now, the people having been in camp at Sinai almost a year, the season for celebration had come, and God commanded Israel to keep Passover, and so to inaugurate that unending succession of Passovers which characterized the history of Israel and has continued even to this day among Jews and Christians, for by the death of Christ the Passover is taken up into the Lord's Supper.

In the Priestly narrative, this second celebration is made the occasion for a law to provide for those who cannot observe the feast at the proper time because they have become unclean by touching a dead person (vss. 6-12; see Num. 19:11-22) or are away on a journey. Keeping Passover was a matter of grave necessity for all Israelites; its omission meant that they were left outside the community's renewal of its identity in God's deliverance. By divine permission, Moses therefore sets a supplementary Passover on the fourteenth of the second month for all unable to participate in the one held in the first month. Verse 14 states once again the eligibil-

ity of the sojourner—not a "stranger," but a non-Israelite who had
cast his lot with God's people—to share the Passover (see Exod.
12:48). The limits of Israel as the Covenant People were never
strictly ethnic.

God's Guidance in the Wilderness (9:15-23)

According to all the narrative traditions of the Pentateuch,
God's appearance in the awesome cloud of his glory was a constant feature of Israel's life in the wilderness. This cloud constituted the manner in which the invisible transcendent God, upon
whom no man can look, chose to manifest his presence to Israel
in those days. The cloud appeared as Israel left Egypt (Exod. 13:
21-22) to guide the people to his holy mount. It settled upon the
summit of Sinai during the making of the Covenant (Exod. 19:16;
24:15-18). When the Tabernacle was complete, God's glory filled
it; and the cloud became the guide for Israel in her way through
the trackless wilderness.

In Israel's pilgrimage to the Promised Land, she was instructed
by the movement of the cloud, which, becoming fiery at night, was
always visible. When the cloud moved, the people broke camp;
and they stopped at the place where the cloud settled. Their every
move and camp were made in response to the command of the
Lord. In following the cloud, Israel began to learn that her way in
history was a pilgrimage guided by a vision of the glory of God.

The Trumpets of the Lord (10:1-10)

In the Priestly narrative, the last event in Israel's preparation
to leave Sinai was the making of the two sacred trumpets to be
used to give the signals which would direct the host of Israel as
they broke camp and marched through the wilderness. These
trumpets were slender metal tubes a cubit in length, with flaring
mouths. The pair of trumpets was used later in Israel's life in Canaan to signal the beginning of festivals, to mark the offering of
sacrifice, and to assemble Israel's army for battle. This story as-
cribes their role to the original institutions at Sinai, set up by Moses
at the command of the Lord. The sound of the trumpets was a memorial, a "remembrance" before God; the blast went forth as a
flourishing musical prayer to God and as a reminder to Israel of
God's oversight of them.

The Departure from Sinai (Num. 10:11-28)

According to the Priestly chronology, Israel broke her camp at Sinai thirteen months and twenty days after the Exodus from Egypt; she had been at Sinai some ten months (vs. 11; see Exod. 19:1). The signal for the departure was the movement of the cloud (see Num. 9:15-23), which rose and went before them and "settled down" in the wilderness of Paran, a region in the eastern central section of the peninsula of Sinai. This was the first of a long series of marches and encampments, stages of a journey always directed by the command of the Lord through Moses.

The tribes set out according to the order already arranged in chapters 1-2, with the Levites carrying the Tabernacle in the center of the column (see chs. 3-4). The order of march, as well as the arrangement of the camp, was a testimony to Israel's identity; they were twelve tribes, the People of the Lord, in whose midst was the dwelling of God.

IN THE WILDERNESS: ISRAEL'S PILGRIMAGE TO THE LAND OF PROMISE
Numbers 10:29—21:35

The second major section of Numbers tells of Israel's years in the wilderness. These chapters describe how Israel left her camp at Sinai, marched to the southern boundaries of Canaan, failed in an assault upon its inhabitants, spent a generation in the wilderness, circled to the east, and made camp in the plains of Moab. Most of the narratives deal with events belonging to the first and the last parts of this journey. The long stretch of years in the middle is illuminated by only a few stories. The section is composed of material which comes from the two earliest epics of Israel (J and E), set in a framework furnished by the Priestly history.

It is the story of the journey to the edge of the Jordan and of what happened during the forty years in the wilderness which furnishes the unity and continuity for the various episodes in this section. But there is far more here than the geography of Israel's route from Sinai to Canaan. The majority of the stories have an inner consistency of theme which becomes almost monotonous in its terrible repetition. It is the theme of "murmuring." No sooner has

Israel reached the first camp (11:1-3) than a complaint breaks out among the people at the hardships of the wilderness. Israel laments the rigorous reality of the pilgrimage to which the Lord had summoned her, and the sound of petulant rebellious murmuring against the Lord and his leader, Moses, becomes the dolorous accompaniment to the march. After Taberah the motif continues at Kibroth-hattaavah (11:4-35), in the ill-fated attempt to enter Canaan from the south (chs. 13-14), at Meribah (20:1-13), and in the story of the fiery serpents (21:4-9). And there are two more stories which are distinctive because they tell about attempts to overthrow the authority of the leader(s) ordained by the Lord, the rebellion of Miriam and Aaron against Moses (ch. 12) and the revolt of Korah (ch. 16).

The theme is not new. It has already appeared in the first sequence of stories about the march through the wilderness, the journey from Egypt to Sinai in Exodus 13-18. At the moment of their great deliverance at the Reed Sea (Exod. 14:10-12), Israel in panic at the approach of Pharaoh's chariots taunted Moses bitterly, "For it would have been better for us to serve the Egyptians than to die in the wilderness." Then, in the very face of the Lord's manifestation of his power, the murmuring began in the wilderness—at Marah (Exod. 15:22-25), in the manna story (Exod. 16), and at Rephidim (Exod. 17). Thus, the entire wilderness epic *in its dimension as a story of Israel* is a sorry tale of a weak, complaining, faithless folk.

What is the lesson of this scathing honesty, this depreciation of Israel, the self-portrait of a people which lacks every element of ethnic heroism? It asserts with inescapable clarity the fact that the power and the glory belong to God, and not to man. The Lord is the true subject of this history, not the people. The way through the wilderness is not won by the bravery or character or religious genius of Israel, but rather by the faithfulness and devotion of God. Israel has no claim to make for herself; she exists wholly in the love and action of God—a point which Moses makes tirelessly in the opening chapters of Deuteronomy (chs. 6-11). The holy history is a witness to God; it points to the Church only as the sphere of his intervention in this world.

The second general point of the sequence follows from the first. The Covenant is the institution of a relationship in which God deals with sinners. This truth has two sides. On the one hand, it keeps Israel from assuming any status which has its own right and justification. The Covenant community does not acquire any independent holiness, is not its own end, it has no separate power or righteousness to offer the world, it is not a "redemptive community." It is a community of sinners who never approach God or live under him except in recognition and confession of their sin. Said Aaron to Moses at Sinai, "You know the people, that they are set on evil" (Exod. 32:22). Said God to Moses, "Say to the people of Israel, 'You are a stiff-necked people' " (Exod. 33:5). Said Moses to Israel at the Jordan, "You have been rebellious against the LORD from the day that I knew you" (Deut. 9:24). These accusations point to the reality of which the wilderness stories are the record. The Covenant creates no super-race. The way of the Church is not pride and self-assertion, but humility and repentance.

On the other hand, these stories proclaim the message of grace —that the sin of the Church does not frustrate the will of God to bless. Time and time again the judgment and forgiveness of God overcome the rebellion of Israel. In his wrath God sets up a barrier against Israel's rebellion, and in his steadfast love he opens a door on the future. Israel cannot escape God, for he will not let them go. He humbled them; he let them hunger that he might feed them. He taught them that man does not live by bread alone, but by everything that proceeds out of the mouth of the Lord. As a man disciplines his son, so the Lord disciplined Israel (Deut. 8: 1-6). What unfolds in this panorama is not so much the way of Israel as the way of the Lord with his people. And because it is God's way, the Church must heed the admonition of the Apostle Paul and apply these stories to itself: "These things are warnings for us . . . written down for our instruction . . . Therefore let any one who thinks that he stands take heed lest he fall" (I Cor. 10: 6-12).

The stories of murmuring and rebellion do not, however, exhaust the section, even though they characterize it. The collection of instructions for various ritual observances (ch. 15) gives no hint why the arrangers of the Pentateuch placed it at its present location. Nor does the chapter on the ritual of the red cow for purification (ch. 19). In the latter part of the section, Israel once again begins to move with purpose; the wandering resumes the directional thrust of a pilgrimage. Edom blocks Israel's way to the east (20:14-29), but after a victory over Arad (21:1-9) she makes her way around the Dead Sea to the Jordan area (21:10-

20). The victory over Sihon and Og (21:21-35) makes room for her camp in the plains of Moab (ch. 21) and clears territory which some of the tribes are to settle. In a real sense, the Conquest has already begun and in spite of herself Israel is on the threshold of the land of her destiny.

A Guide for the Wilderness (Num. 10:29-32)

Facing the many problems of finding a way through the trackless wilderness and surviving in its arid land, Moses turns again to the clan of his wife, Zipporah. The Midianites were wandering nomads who lived in this wilderness and knew its routes and camping places. They had come to meet Israel at Sinai (Exod. 18), and now wanted to return to their own territory. Moses promises that, if they will accompany Israel, they will share in the promise of God. The benefits of the election history are open to those who will join the People of God and serve in their pilgrimage. Though this passage does not report their answer, Moses' in-laws were persuaded by him and shared in the Promised Land (Judges 1:16; 4:11).

The narrative of J and E takes up again in this passage, after last appearing in Exodus 34. The J source calls Moses' father-in-law "Reuel" (Exod. 2:18). E uses "Jethro" (Exod. 18). Numbers 10:29 could mean that Hobab was Moses' brother-in-law or father-in-law (see Judges 4:11). About this name, the early tradition is unclear; probably several ethnic facets of Israel's early history are fused into the figure so variously named. Here the ethnic name is "Midianite," but elsewhere "Kenite" (Judges 1:16; 4:11). "Midian" may be the name of a larger tribal family, of which the Kenites were a group.

The Ark of the Lord (Num. 10:33-36)

Israel's departure from Sinai, of which the Priestly narrative's detailed report has already been given (10:11-28), is now described by the older JE history. Led by the Ark of the Lord, Israel goes for three days before camping again, presumably at Taberah (11:3). The cloud of the Lord, manifesting his presence, is over them as they go (see 9:15-23).

The Ark was a portable shrine, an empty throne for the invisible King who reigned over the tribes as their sole Lord. Israel believed that when the Ark was moved, God arose and went before his people; when it was still, God returned and sat enthroned in their midst. Verses 35 and 36 record the ancient ritual cries which interpreted the meaning of the Ark's movement (see Ps. 68:1). The Ark led the people through the wilderness and into Canaan (Joshua 3:1-6) and was particularly important in the battles of Israel, where it represented God's leadership and participation in the "holy war" by which the "holy history" won its way.

Murmuring at Taberah (Num. 11:1-3)

The story of Taberah introduces the narrative about Israel in the wilderness. It is one of the frequent accounts of Israel's complaints because of the hardships of their way when they followed God. These stories of murmuring in the wilderness lie around the account of Sinai like a dramatic parenthesis; they appear in Exodus between the Reed Sea and Sinai (Exod. 14-19), and now resume to characterize the wilderness narrative.

This passage reads like a summation of the rest. The story has no circumstances to explain its bare report; it is rather a formula for the constant theme and variations worked out in fuller detail in the subsequent stories of complaint, murmuring, and rebellion. No sooner has Israel reached her first camp, three days from Sinai, than she finds the pilgrimage difficult and hard. She complains before the Lord. The Lord is angry and sends his divine fire to burn among them (see also I Kings 18:38; II Kings 1:10, 12). The people cry out to Moses, Moses intercedes with the Lord, and the fire abates. The camp is given a name that commemorates the experience: Taberah means "burning."

The meaning of this type of story will be explored in the cases where the account is filled out (for example, 11:4-35). Suffice it to say here that Israel had the fixation, common to all religions, which associated God with success. She wanted her religion to "work."

Craving at Kibroth-hattaavah (Num. 11:4-35)

Although the account includes no report of Israel's departure from Taberah, the incident reported here occurs at another camp site, named because of what happened there; "Kibroth-hattaavah"

means "the graves of those who craved." The narrative belongs
to the JE story, which here is composed of various elements fused
into one sequence in the preliterary stage of tradition. In the present form the story has two dramatic themes: the restless, faithless
dissatisfaction of Israel and the frustration of Moses as their
leader. The story lets us see both People of God and God's leader
more clearly in their relationship to him.

The weeping of Israel is a failure of faith in God. The rabble
with them (non-Israelite people enslaved in Egypt, who escaped
with Israel) precipitated the discontent, and Israel took up their
complaint. With the great events of the Exodus and Sinai behind
them and the Promised Land still ahead, they yearned for the
diet of Egypt. In the wilderness they were free but lived on Spar-
tan fare. Now the food of slavery seemed better than the fare of
freedom. Craving of flesh for flesh overwhelmed them. The Old
Testament Church expressed in tears its preference for slavery to
the world, so as to share its paltry pleasures, rather than suffering
in the campaign by which the world was to be overcome. They
even despised the food which God provided. "There is nothing at
all but this manna," they wailed (see Exod. 16:4-36). How easy
it is for the Church at the Lord's Table to think that his provision
is not enough! To demand what God does not give is to reject the
Lord who is in the midst of the Church (vs. 20). It is tantamount
to rebellion against the whole enterprise of salvation. For the
sake of meat Israel forgot the deliverance of God: "Why did we
come forth out of Egypt?"

When God's anger blazed hotly at Israel, Moses showed how
human he was and how treacherously difficult it is for a man to
lead a faithless people in faith. Moses' faith failed too, and he
made his own complaint to God (vss. 11-15). Faced with Israel's
frustrating vacillation and the Lord's displeasure, he felt trapped
between them. He could not bring off his mission; suddenly his
calling to lead Israel became a burden which he could not bear,
for he felt utterly alone. Israel's failure corrupted his own sense
of the power of God. He did not ask for help; he prayed for death,
in a prayer for escape which is in its own way a rebellion against
the commission of God. Even when God said that he, God, would
give Israel the meat they craved, Moses protested that *he* did not
know where *he,* Moses, would get the meat (vss. 18-23). Moses,
who was the bringer of God's word, had also to learn again that
God's power was not diminished. His word would come to pass.

The answer to Moses' loneliness in his office comes in the gift of "the spirit" upon the seventy elders (vss. 16-17, 24-29), perhaps the same seventy who shared the Covenant meal with him at Sinai (Exod. 24:9-11). At God's direction, Moses selected seventy who were recognized as leaders in their own tribes and brought them to the Tent of Meeting. God endowed them with the spirit of office which he had given to Moses. As the sign of their endowment, the elders "prophesied." The expression here means that they were seized with the kind of Spirit-filled ecstasy which later possessed the early prophets (I Sam. 10:10-12; 19:20-24) as a sign and equipment of their zeal for the Lord. Now Moses would not bear the burden of this people alone; those elders would stand with Moses in the task of keeping Israel in faithfulness. Even two who remained in the camp were given the gift of the Spirit. When Joshua was jealous for Moses' sake because Eldad and Medad seemed to prophesy independently of Moses, Moses said, "Would that all the LORD's people were prophets, that the LORD would put his spirit upon them!" Moses' desire that every man should live in the strength of his own zeal for the Lord, needing no man to bear him as a burden, is put in an exclamation which reaches out to the Pentecost when God's Spirit would fall on all the Church (Acts 2; Joel 2:28-32).

And the people get their meat. A wind from the Lord brings great flocks of quail, birds whose large migratory flights still occur along the Sinai peninsula, and they fall around the camp. The birds come in such quantity that the people's craving turns to loathing. While they were yet in their orgy of satisfying their craving, a plague from the Lord fell upon them. Israel learned both the power of God to help and his wrath against their faithlessness.

The Revolt of Miriam and Aaron (Num. 12:1-16)

The murmuring and dissatisfaction of Israel with Moses and the Lord here breaks out in the very family of Moses. In this JE story Miriam and Aaron, in jealous ambition, speak against the prominent position of Moses. The immediate occasion for their hostility is said to be the Cushite woman whom Moses had married. To whom "Cushite" refers, and why the marriage was offensive, must remain tantalizingly obscure. Cushite usually means "Ethiopian" in the Old Testament, but we know of no other wife to Moses than Zipporah, who was a Kenite or Midianite (Exod. 2:15-22). There is the outside possibility that the name "Cush" may have covered the tribes of North Arabia and so could be a different way of referring to Zipporah. But whatever the mystery about Moses' wife, she was not the real issue which provoked Moses' brother and sister. They were overcome by that jealousy of prerogative and office and eminence which has been the scourge of the Church and the source of many divisions in all ages. Miriam was a prophetess (Exod. 15:20) and Aaron the spokesman for Israel (Exod. 4:14-16). Because the Lord spoke through them, they had come to resent the unique role of leadership which Moses played in Israel. They turned the work which they had been given by God into an attack upon the work given to Moses. They took the gift of office as their own right to be first; not the *work,* but the *person,* became the issue.

The comment that Moses was the meekest of all men puts him in utter contrast to their ambition and jealousy. "Meek" does not mean obsequious or hypocritically self-effacing; it is the quality of humility, the mark of the man who does not justify himself but depends eagerly and willingly on God. The self which is humbled before God is the selflessness that God wills to use: "Blessed are the meek, for they shall inherit the earth" (Matt. 5:5).

God, hearing what Miriam and Aaron say, intervenes to justify Moses, who does not defend himself. All three are summoned to the Tent of Meeting, where God appears in the cloud to deal with the rebellion. The Lord's words to the two are given in the form of an oracular poem (vss. 6-8), although the poetic form does not appear in the printed English text. The gist of the poem is a comparison between the way in which God communicates with the prophet and the way he speaks with Moses. The revelation to the prophet is indirect and somewhat opaque; it comes in the symbolism of a vision or in the events of a dream, or in a riddle. But with Moses it is otherwise. Because Moses is entrusted with responsibility for all Israel, revelation comes to him in a way that is unique to his office. God speaks to him "mouth to mouth," which means directly and personally, without the media of symbols (see also "face to face" in Exod. 33:11). What Moses sees is "the form of the LORD"—the very aspect by which the Lord is manifest—and not objects which merely symbolize his person. No other man, even though the Lord speak through him, is given such personal and intimate directness of commerce with the Lord.

So the Mosaic revelation has an authenticity and authority which make it pre-eminent over all others in Israel.

Because the poem contrasts Moses and a prophet, not mentioning Miriam and Aaron, its cogency depends on the supposition that the two functioned as prophets. Moreover, the poem has a particular kind of prophet in mind—primarily the "seer," the type of prophet exemplified in Samuel, and not the later "writing prophets." Whatever its historical roots in the wilderness time, this story was particularly relevant in Israel during the time of the Judges and the early kings, when the "seer" was prominent. The clear teaching of Moses is made definitive for the work of the seer; his work was under the authority of the Mosaic faith. One can feel in the poem the struggle to keep the seer in line with the Mosaic faith, and to fend off the pagan influences which might have entered Israel's religion through the seers' mystical activity. (Paul's struggle with those who speak in tongues in the Early Church is an analogy. See I Corinthians 12-14.)

God's rebuke falls on Miriam alone; why, the story does not say. When the cloud is removed, she has leprosy, a disease which means that she is unclean and has to be put outside the camp, away from the People of God. She who claimed the first place in jealousy now has no place in the People of God. Aaron, shattered when he sees his sister, turns to the brother whom he had attacked, and calls Moses "my lord." Moses once again shows his selflessness. No bitterness or resentment blocks his response, and he prays for Miriam. In his meekness, authority and mercy are wed; he is not there for himself, but for God and for the people.

Miriam is healed, but by divine decree she must spend seven days outside the camp as one who is unclean. The reference to a father's spitting in the face of his daughter draws on an old socio-legal custom; to spit in another's face in a public court was a severe ritual of rebuke and rejection (Deut. 25:9). Miriam's leprosy was not to be taken less seriously than such a rebuke of a father to his daughter. When Miriam's seclusion was over, Israel left Hazeroth (see 11:35) and journeyed to the wilderness of Paran (an area which the P narrative assumed as having been gained in 10:12). Paran is the region in the eastern central sector of the peninsula of Sinai, and includes Kadesh-barnea within its area.

The Failure to Enter the Promised Land
(Num. 13:1—14:45)

When Israel had reached Kadesh in the wilderness of Paran
(13:26), she was poised on the threshold of the consummation
toward which God had been moving her history since the call of
Abraham. But Israel did not enter Canaan. Instead, there took
place that tragic blunder for which all Israel's other failures in
the wilderness had been an ominous preparation. Her faith failed
at the moment of consummation. First, she refused to go with
God, and then she tried to take the land without him. The whole
story is a testimony to the Church in all times that the People of
God can make their way through history to the fulfillment only
by faith in the power of God's presence in their midst.

Chapters 13 and 14 are a combination of the JE epic and the
P history. The careful reader easily detects the presence of two
fairly complete narrative strands which have been interwoven.
Each tells the same basic story, but there are differences of detail as well as repetition. In the JE strand, the spies start from
Kadesh, explore only the southern region around Hebron, and
report that the land is fertile; and Caleb figures as the advocate
of courageous attack. In P, the name of the camping area is the
wilderness of Paran, the spies survey the entire land of Palestine,
and they report that the land is barren; and Joshua appears along-
side Caleb. The repetition in the two strands is clearest in the
two accounts of God's verdict on the faithless people (JE in 14:
20-25 and P in 14:26-35). The two fused stories are meant to
be read as one, with each contributing its interpretation of the
meaning of this episode. Speaking in terms of bare external history, what happened was that Israel tried to attack Canaan from
the south, was defeated by the inhabitants of the Negeb, and lived
for a generation at a stalemate around Kadesh. The biblical story
is concerned with the inner history as well, that is, with what
transpired between Israel and God and what happened to the
corporate soul of Israel as the Elect People.

The narrative begins with a report of the selection of the
spies (13:1-17a, from P). At the command of God, Moses picks
a leader from each of the twelve tribes according to the classic
pattern for every enterprise of Israel; each tribe participates
through its leader. The names are given in the same type of report

which appears in the census arrangements (1:1-16; 34:17-28; see also 7:12-83). The names are not the same as in the two foregoing lists; obviously the Priestly tradition assumes that the office of "leader" was held in each tribe by more than one man. Joshua (who was introduced in the JE narrative of Exod. 17:9) is selected as the "leader" from Ephraim (vs. 8). His name is given as "Hoshea" ("salvation"); but Moses is said to have changed it by the addition of the divine proper name to Joshua ("the LORD is salvation") (vs. 16). The divine name, which was not known before the revelation to Moses (Exod. 6:2-3), is set upon a man whose life spans the wilderness and the conquest, a foreshadowing of the role Joshua is to play in the future.

In Deuteronomy 1:22-25 it is the people who initiate the scouting party, with the purpose of exploring the best route into the land. P attributes the initiation to God, and has probably displaced the JE opening of the story. But the purpose of the spies in the older narrative is clearly put in verses 17b-20. The spies were to determine whether the land to the north was desirable and how strongly it was held. Moses' instructions about bringing back some fruit of the land may indicate his intention to spur the flagging spirits of Israel with evidences of a far better land than the wilderness in which they lingered.

The spies were directed to explore the Negeb and the hill country. The Negeb is the arid, broken terrain between Beer-sheba and Kadesh-barnea. Here "the hill country" certainly means the mountainous terrain of Judah around Hebron and may include the central hill country around Jerusalem and beyond. Hebron is the only city mentioned in the report of the explorations. Verse 21 (from P) says that the spies went as far as Rehob, an unknown site, which according to the text was near the entrance of Hamath, and so must have been in the extreme north of the sources of the Jordan River. In one of the fertile valleys near Hebron, the Israelites cut a branch of a grapevine whose clusters were extremely large. The name of the valley was Eshcol, which means "cluster," and Hebrew tradition associated the name with the spies' journey.

In verses 25-33 the spies return and make their report. On the facts they are agreed: the land is good but is strongly held by its present inhabitants. The land, they said, is one that "flows with milk and honey," an idiom for extreme fertility, often applied to the Promised Land. In ancient mythology, milk and honey were

said to be the food of the gods, and the idiom casts an aura of un-
imagined richness over the land. But the territory was already
held by numerous peoples living in large, fortified cities. The
Amalekites, a wandering nomadic people, were already settling
the fringes of the Negeb. The Canaanites, a northwestern Semitic
people, had long since spread from the north into the fertile
coastal plain and into the northern Jordan Valley. The Amorites
were to the south of them in the Jordan Valley and shared the
central hill country with such Hurrian groups as the Jebusites and
Hittites. The description is an essentially accurate picture of
Palestine before the conquest, when the land was occupied by a
variety of peoples organized around small city states. The "descendants of Anak," mentioned in verses 22, 28, and 33 as particularly fearsome because of their size, are a special problem.
These residents of Hebron were said to be the descendants of the
legendary giants called Nephilim (Gen. 6:4).

Though the spies agreed on the facts, they were seriously divided in their judgment. Caleb and Joshua (14:6, 30) were confident that Israel could take the land; they did not overestimate
the difficulties, because they did not underestimate the power of
the Lord. But the rest of the spies could see only the strength of
their adversaries. In their lack of faith they could see no reality
but the visible problem, no possibility except what their own
strength could accomplish. They said of themselves that they felt
like grasshoppers before the strength of the people of the land.
According to P's contribution here (vs. 32), they went so far in
their fear as to falsify their picture of the land, calling it barren
and dangerous. Cowardice led them to see the very Land of
Promise, the goal of their pilgrimage, as empty of all attraction
and a real danger.

The reaction of the people to the spies' report is described in
14:1-10a. In the light of their previous conduct in the face of
any difficulty, there could hardly be any doubt as to which of
the two interpretations by the spies they would accept. Almost
eagerly they believed the worst, and we hear once again the
wearying lament of the faithless mob (Exod. 16:2; 17:3; 32:1;
Num. 11:1, 4-6): "the people wept . . . and . . . murmured." "All
the congregation raised a loud cry"; what a contradiction—the
folk who had become "the congregation" by the mighty act of
the Lord against the ancient East's greatest empire now lamenting
because Canaanites and Amorites stood in their way. How easy it

always is for the Church to view the hard realities of its present as more difficult than those past dangers through which God has brought his people! The spies' fear infects the people like a virulent contagion, and immediately their apprehensions become their certain future: "Our wives and our little ones will become a prey." They even go so far as to accuse God, changing his purpose of blessing into one of murder (vs. 3). And so they say, "Back to Egypt!" They will replace God's leader with one whom they choose, and so undo the entire "holy history" and turn back the purpose of God. Now they think they prefer slavery under the powers of this world with its apparent security rather than freedom under God with its awesome responsibility.

Faced with such incredible faithlessness, Moses and Aaron are distraught and fall to the ground in humblest prayer, knowing that this people has blasphemed God. Caleb and Joshua speak the word of faith which belongs to the true Israel: "The LORD is with us; do not fear." That fact is greater than any foe, the fact of election and Covenant. All depends on the Lord; if he delights in Israel, he will bring them in. But the fearful proposals of Israel endanger the very Covenant. They are rebelling against their Lord. The only response of the people to this witness of faith by Joshua and Caleb is to take up stones to stone them, as later a mob would take up stones against another witness when he pointed the way toward the fulfillment (Acts 7:57-60).

In verses 10b-12 the Lord intervenes to deal with Israel's rebellion. The Tabernacle is suddenly covered with the glory of the Lord, the luminous cloud by which God manifested his presence to Israel when he would confront them as the Lord in their midst. The questions which God addresses to Moses are not interrogatory, but rhetorical accusations. What happens here can go on no longer. The people in their fear despise the Lord; all the signs he has wrought for their sake (the wonders by which he brought them out of Egypt and kept them in the wilderness) have not brought them to faith, to that personal trust and reliance on the Lord which it is always his purpose to call forth in his acts of salvation. A people without faith cannot be the People of God. As things stand, Israel's way is at an end. Israel had come to expect only death, so the Lord will give it. He will prosecute his purpose now through Moses, who will become a second Abram with whom God will begin all over. He will make "a nation" of Moses (see Gen. 12:1-3).

Moses' reply to this verdict of God is given in verses 13-19. The reply is a strange and perplexing combination of meekness and daring. Moses does not so much as consider the great honor proposed by God; rather, he shows once again that selflessness in which he is identified with Israel and yet wholly devoted to God. The daring comes in the way he responds, for he even ventures to advise and counsel God himself as to what ought to be done. Moses makes two distinct appeals. Neither makes any excuse for Israel or discounts in any way the evil of the people's rebellion. Both are appeals to the revealed nature of God and are based on what God has already made known concerning himself. Therein lies the secret of this strange intercession, in which Moses stands in the breach before God to turn away his wrath from destroying his people (Ps. 106:23).

Moses rests his first appeal on the glory of God (vss. 13-16). If God destroys this people, within whose history he has manifested his action and presence, then his purpose to reveal himself as Lord of history (Exod. 9:16; 15:14-18) will be frustrated; the surrounding nations who know that the Lord is Israel's God will attribute their death to his lack of power to complete what he began. Through the election, God has an involvement in the destiny of the Church; his glory is at stake. (For other cases of God's glory as a basis for his help to the Church in its sin, see Isaiah 48:11; 52:5-6; Ezekiel 36:16-36; 39:21-29.) Then Moses appeals to the power of God to forgive (vss. 17-19). He recites the revelation which God had given of himself at Sinai (Exod. 34:6-7). There Moses, fearing to go with such a sinful people without the assurance that they would be sustained by the Lord's pardon (Exod. 34:9), had prayed for forgiveness for this "stiff-necked people." Israel's ultimate hope in her sin was the greatness of God's "steadfast love," that is, that will to maintain the Covenant relation against all difficulties which belongs to the divine nature. That power and freedom to forgive is the divine possibility in which the "holy history" rests forever.

Here is the profound mystery of intercession—that God allows his will to be sought and shaped on earth as well as in heaven. Intercession must seek what is in the revealed nature of God. Yet, by God's grace, chosen men of faith become, as it were, co-authors of his will. In this case Moses plays a mediatorial role. He is a man so empty of self and zealous for God's glory and purpose that his plea does no violence to the divine sovereignty.

He is the one point of contact for God within Israel. The faith of the just, holding up the sins and needs of the people, yet seeking only the glory of God, is the true possibility on earth of the union of God's glory and mercy among men. In this intercessory office Moses fashions and prepares for the intercessory mediation of the Christ who, in the sacrifice of self, accomplishes God's glory and our forgiveness.

The Lord gives his answer to Moses in verses 20-25. Once again he grants forgiveness to Israel. The crucial place of Moses' intercession is seen in that it is the "word" of Moses which God himself cites as the reason for the pardon (vs. 20); this one chosen man by his intercession keeps the election alive for the entire people. The effect of God's pardon for Israel is that they remain alive, untouched by God's wrath. Moreover, God gives them their own desire; they had feared to enter the Land of Promise, so they will remain in the wilderness. The present generation of Israelites had beheld the glory of God's presence and seen the wonder of his works; yet their response had been to put God "to the proof" (that is, to respond in disbelief and dissatisfaction) and to fail to obey. Verse 22 refers to ten occasions on which Israel had tempted God; "ten" here probably is the number of complete and full measure, but if one allows the manna incident in Exodus 16 to count for two, there are ten murmuring and rebellion stories in all. In any case, Israel has finally refused to play her role as the Covenant People of faith; so the advance of the history of God's people has to await another generation. Caleb, as one of the believers, is excepted from the verdict. The final word of the Lord is, "Set out for the wilderness." The Promised Land is not for those who have no faith.

In 14:26-38 the Priestly counterpart to 14:20-25 (JE) is given. It is wholly concerned with the verdict of God that Israel must remain in the wilderness until the present adult generation is dead. The particular genius of this section is the way in which everything is made to balance out in a complex of correspondences, and every consequence is specifically and quantitatively drawn. The adults had said they would die in the wilderness; this will happen (vss. 28-29). Their little ones, who they feared would become a prey, will know the land their elders despised (vs. 31). The spies were gone forty days; the term in the wilderness will be forty years (vs. 34). The faithless spies who caused the trouble will die. Joshua and Caleb who spoke the word of faith will live.

The Priestly theologian shows how Israel's punishment unfolds out of the particularity of their sin; God's wrath is not arbitrary emotion; it is the exact recognition of the sin of men.

But the tragic drama of failure is not complete. Verses 39-45 tell how a vacillating Israel, on hearing the verdict of God, undertook to repair their failure in their own way. They will do in remorse what they had failed to do in faith: they will claim the promise in their own time, in their own way (vs. 40). They do not go as the People of the Lord, but as a willful, undisciplined mob. The crucial features of "holy war" are absent; neither Moses nor the Ark leaves the camp, and the Lord is not with them. This belated assault on the hill country is no less than a final paroxysm of disobedience. The Amalekites and Canaanites defeat them easily and pursue them as far as Hormah, a site possibly to the northeast of Beer-sheba. The story stands as a testimony that the only identity in which the Elect People can fulfill the purpose of God is that of a believing, obedient community. The "holy history" is not the story of the people, but of God's work through the people.

A Collection of Material on Ritual Observances (Num. 15:1-41)

This chapter contains five sections, each of which deals with some ritual practice of Israel's religion. The first four are instructions in the familiar Priestly style; the fifth is a story which emphasizes the crucial importance of the Sabbath law. All seem to come from P, although there is evidence that some of the material is derived from H. The five sections have no internal similarity to indicate why they are grouped together. Nor is there presupposed any connection with the story of Israel to show why the collection appears just after Israel's failure to enter Canaan in chapters 13-14.

On Some Uses of Cereal and Drink Offerings (15:1-16)

These regulations do not replace those concerning the presentation of cereal offerings as a separate ritual (Lev. 2; 6:14-18) but rather specify the amounts of fine flour, oil, and wine to be brought with burnt offerings and sacrifices of peace offerings, whether presented individually or at appointed feasts. The regulations list the portions for a lamb (vss. 4-5), ram (vss. 6-7), and bull (vss. 8-9), with the amounts increasing in relation to the size of the animal. Flour is measured by the ephah (about one bushel); oil and wine by the hin (about one and one-half gallons). The drink offering, according to the apocryphal Book of Ecclesiasticus (50:15), was poured at the foot of the altar. Flour, oil, and wine made up, along with the meat, the basic items of a Semite's diet, and they were used from earliest times in sacrificial ritual. The careful specification of amounts probably comes from around the sixth century and belongs to the Priestly history. In Ezekiel 46:5-7 there is a similar regulation which gives every sign of being an earlier form of these in Numbers. Verses 14-16 state that this law applies to the "sojourner" as well as to the Israelite. The sojourner was a person who, without being a recognized resident and member of Israel, was granted certain rights and status in social and religious life.

On Offering the First of the Coarse Meal (15:17-21)

This regulation seems to belong to those laws dealing with the sacrifice of "firstlings" (see Exod. 13:11-16). The word translated "coarse meal" may mean "dough in the first stage of preparation." From the dough made of the first grain coming from the threshing floor at harvest a contribution is to be set aside for the Lord.

On Sacrifices for Sins Done Unwittingly (15:22-31)

These regulations describe the sacrifices which are to be brought by the whole congregation of Israel (vss. 22-26) or an individual (vss. 27-31), whether Israelite or sojourner, when sin has been committed unwittingly. For the congregation a young bull as a burnt offering and a male goat as a sin offering were required; for an individual, a female goat as a sin offering. By the sin offering, atonement was effected and forgiveness granted by God. This section ought to be compared with Leviticus 4:1—5:13 (see comment). The terms "unwittingly" and "err" ("error") probably covered violations of ritual law by mistake, errors in the administration of justice, and possibly those situations in which misfortune raised the suspicion that divine punishment had come upon people or individuals for an unknown sin. Verses 30-31 specifically exclude from atonement and forgiveness those sins committed "with a high hand," that is, sins committed in knowing, willful, bold defiance of God's commandments. So to sin was to revile the Lord and despise his word. In old Israel such an attitude made the very Covenant relationship impossible. The faith of Israel regarded outright rebellion and rejection of the authority of the Covenant Lord in utter seriousness. In the Christian faith no sin is excluded from forgiveness because of atonement in Jesus Christ, except blasphemy against the Holy Spirit (Mark 3:28-30; see I John 5:16-17). Perhaps this sin has a proper theological analogy to the sin committed with a high hand. In between sins committed by mistake and outright rejection of God's authority lay a whole range of sins done in weakness, which may be covered by the term "unwittingly."

The Punishment of a Sabbathbreaker (15:32-36)

This brief story describes a particular case of a sin committed "with a high hand" (15:30). It appears to be an early *midrash*, that is, a comment on the text by way of illustration; it is of the same type as the story in Leviticus 24:10-23. In Exodus 31:14-15 and 35:2 Sabbathbreaking is made a capital offense. The issue here is how the sentence is to be carried out. The New Testament also teaches that the wages of sin is death (Rom. 6:23). This story warns us of how serious is willful sin in the Covenant community and revives in us a dependence on Christ, whose death is punishment in our place.

A Reminder of the Lord's Commandments (15:37-41)

Following the regulations concerning sacrifice for sins done unwittingly is this ordinance for a continual reminder to Israel of the Lord's commandments. The people are to wear tassels bound to the corners of their garments by a blue thread to call to mind their unending obligation to obedience. These tassels were worn by Jews in New Testament times; Jesus wore them (Mark 6:56), and the Pharisees exaggerated them in great ostentation (Matt. 23:5). The constant danger for the People of the Lord is that they will follow their own eyes and heart, out of which comes evil (Mark 7:21-23), and will not fix their mind singly and in purity upon their Savior Lord, whose will is to be the only goal of the life of faith.

The Rebellion of Korah (Num. 16:1-50)

At first reading this long chapter seems to tell of a rebellion of the Levites led by Korah against the sole right of Aaron to the priestly office. But closer inspection easily shows that "the rebellion of Korah" is composed of stories about, not one incident, but two. Two stories with different details, but with similar themes (the revolt of a group against divinely constituted authority), have here been merged in the final written form of the Bible. The second story has in turn been expanded, so that its meaning applies to a further problem in Israel's religious life. As it stands the chapter is an excellent example of the living quality of the Word in Israel's religious history, before the Old Testament was written in its final form. The meaning of an early story became God's guidance in a later situation, and its relevance in the later situation became part of the historical tradition. It will help to clarify what the material of the chapter means if we deal with each strand separately.

The earliest story tells of the revolt of the Reubenites, Dathan and Abiram. It comes from the J material though some interpreters detect touches of E also. Its material appears in these verses: 1b-2a, 12-15, 25-26, 27b-34 (omitting 32b). It is this earlier story of Dathan and Abiram which Deuteronomy knows (Deut. 11:6).

The story begins with the fact of the rebellion. Dathan and Abiram rose up against Moses, having attracted some accomplices in their conspiracy; we are not told who, or how many. On, the son of Peleth, who is their associate in the revolt, is not mentioned again in the chapter or elsewhere in the Old Testament. Moses, apparently learning of their conspiracy, sends for them to appear before God and the assembly. The conspirators refuse forthrightly and announce the cause of their resentment and resistance. They reject the authority of Moses, because they blame the hardships and failures of the wilderness on him. This attack on Moses is a continuation of the proposal in the spy story to displace him as head of the people (Num. 14:4). Now that Israel has been unable to enter the Promised Land, they consider his leadership bankrupt. As they see it, Moses' sole authority rested in his capacity to get for them the good things of Canaan. The doors seem closed on that land, and they all face death in the wilderness. In their frustrated resentment they even describe Egypt by the favorite phrase for the Promised Land. It was "a land flowing with milk and honey" which they had left. Why should Moses make himself a "prince" over them? They will let him pull the wool over their eyes no longer. They will tolerate an authority only if it gets them what they want, no matter what the guilt of their own failure may be. Clearly, these men are saying that Moses' authority derives from the people, not from God. The will of the people, not the election of God, will settle the question of authority.

Moses is troubled and indignant; he protests to the Lord that he has never used his authority for his own personal advantage, for he has not seized property nor harmed these men. Moses' petition that the Lord pay no heed to their offering (or gift) may indicate that Dathan and Abiram have proceeded to set up their own private worship center, a dangerous threat to the unity of Israel. It would cast a religious aura around what was really a rebellion against God, a rebellion which cut at the very foundations of the wilderness pilgrimage. If they were to attract a following, the pilgrimage of faith would be over.

Moses goes to the tents of Dathan and Abiram, followed by the elders of Israel (vs. 25). The Spirit has done his work (11: 24-25), and the elders are with Moses in this trouble. Moses warns the congregation not to join with the rebels in their wickedness. Then, he puts the issue which the revolt really raises: are the events in the wilderness the work of the Lord or only Moses' attempt to assert his own authority? (vs. 28). He leaves the issue in the hands of the Lord, whose answer is swift and terrible. The earth with a quakelike convulsion swallows up both families, and they go down alive to Sheol, the nether regions of the dead. This work of God's wrath is a symbolic testimony to the Old Testament Church standing at the point of disintegration. Life and death are at stake in Israel's faithfulness to God's authority. To choose the will and work of God is to choose the only possibility of true life; to reject the lordship of God is to choose that living which leads only to death.

The story about Korah also tells of a revolt against the authority of Moses. But in this narrative Aaron shares the role with Moses as an object of hostility, and the issue is the special prerogative of the Levites, Moses and Aaron, to enter the holy precincts of the Tabernacle. The Korah story comes from the basic narrative of P and is found in verses 1a, 2b-7b, 18-24, 27a, 35, 41-50.

Korah leads a rebellion in which he is joined by two hundred and fifty leaders representing all the tribes of Israel (vs. 2). It begins as a protest against the authority of Moses and Aaron by the leadership of the tribes, an effort by the tribal authorities to deny the prerogatives of any central authority over them. Korah is not a Levite in the original P story. His genealogy in verse 1 has been added in a later revision of the narrative. He may have been the Korah of Caleb's clan mentioned in I Chronicles 2:43. The Levitical Korahites were an important group in the postexilic period; and the writer of Numbers 26:11, assuming that these were the ones dealt with in this story, finds it necessary to point out that they did not all die.

The dissidents state their complaint, and their theology, in verse 3. The rebellion is a lay movement against the clergy, a protest against the cultic specialization of Moses and Aaron, who alone are qualified to act in the sacred ritual of ministering to the Lord. Against a theology which allows only those who by their office are "holy" to do the work of the priest, Korah opposes a lay theology that reckons the entire congregation to be holy so that every man may draw near to the Lord. According to Korah, the special function of Moses and Aaron as Levites is but the sign of personal arrogance by which they exalt themselves above the assembly of the Lord. Why should not the entire assembly be as Moses and Aaron? Of course, Korah's lay theology has a good basis: by the Covenant, Israel became a holy nation, a people separated and consecrated to the worship and service of the Lord (Exod. 19: 6). As Korah says, the Lord is in *their* midst. His theory is that the consecration of the whole extends to each individual, giving everybody the status of "holy." No mediator is necessary; no priesthood, representing people before God, and God to people, is necessary. In Korah's theology the significant center of holiness moves to the people themselves, so that no "holy" one representing the holiness of God over against them is required. But can the people be holy on their own, without some arrangement to recognize and maintain the separate holiness of God? God's own act in electing, not only the people, but also mediators within the people, belies it. As Moses says to Korah (vs. 5), the prerogative of the "holy" one who draws near to God is a matter of the Lord's own election and choice.

So in this story, as in that of Dathan and Abiram, Moses leaves the issue in the hands of the Lord. Korah and his company are directed to test their theology by drawing near to the sanctuary to burn incense, a ritual act reserved for the priests, in order to see whether the Lord will accept them as holy. They undertake the test, and, backed by the whole congregation, they draw near to the Tent of Meeting. At this juncture the glory of the Lord appears to all the people. The Lord announces his intention to consume the whole congregation at that moment, except Moses and Aaron. So great is their sin, so terrible is this presumption against sanctity or this democratic arrogance which will tolerate no mediator between proud self and Holy God! Once again Moses intercedes for Israel (vs. 22; see the comment on 13:1—14:45 for a discussion of intercession); the office which Israel rejects becomes the means of redemption from the judgment of God. Moses pleads with the Lord that he who is God of all men ought not to condemn all these who are led astray by the sin of one man. Profoundly Moses appeals to the Lord as the God of all men, in the very moment that Israel attempts to establish a democracy of common holiness! God directs the congregation to get away from the "dwelling" (in verses 24 and 27 the Hebrew word means the Tabernacle; the names of Korah, Dathan, and Abiram were added to facilitate the merging of the two stories). Then the divine fire comes forth and consumes Korah and his two hundred and fifty associates, who are holding the censers (vs. 35).

Verses 41-50 recount yet another episode which, happening on the day after Korah's rebellion, is but its sequel. In truth, the telling of the story sounds like a tragic replaying of the first day. Within twenty-four hours the rebellion flares up again; the restless contagion of revolt has not been purged with the death of Korah and his company. The people assemble and begin to murmur against Moses and Aaron. They complain that Moses and Aaron "have killed the people of the LORD": once more they attribute the work of God to Moses so that they can reject God by rejecting Moses and make their own status as People of the Lord the sole criterion for authority. The Church threatens to make itself divine! Once more the Lord appears in the cloud of his glory to consume the people in his wrath against their presumption. Once more Moses and Aaron intercede for the people. This time the intercession takes the very form which Korah's arrogance had assumed. God's wrath touches the people as a virulent plague. Aaron, as the true priest, stands in the midst of the people, between the living and the dead, burning incense before God, and so makes "atonement" for the people. (On the term "to atone," see Leviticus 1-7.) Once again it is by the very office whose authority they resent that the people are spared in their sin.

The original story of Korah has been extended by the following verses: 1b, 7c-11, 16-17, 36-40. These additions in effect serve to apply the original story to the struggle of the Levites against the house of Aaron because of its exclusive possession of the priestly office. The lay revolt against Moses and Aaron becomes a heretical revolt against the Aaronic priesthood. The theological principle in both is the same, and the extension of the story shows how Israel's tradition was applied to later situations as they arose.

Korah is a leader of the Levites (vss. 1, 8) who seeks the priesthood (vs. 10), and so would claim a prerogative not given to the Levites in the institution of their office (see 1:47-54), but alone to the family of Aaron (3:5-10). Moses makes it clear that Aaron's priesthood is an ordinance of God (vs. 11), so the murmuring jealousy of the Levites is against the Lord himself. Verses 36-40 relate a sequel to the death of Korah and his company. The censers which they carried, having been sanctified by the divine fire, are collected and made into a covering sheath for the altar. The covering becomes a *sign* to Israel (and here is the unmistakable point of the extended story) that only the descendants of Aaron shall draw near as priests before the Lord (vs. 40).

In these two stories and in the extension of the second, there is one single word to the Church of God. The focus of authority and mediation which God ordains within history as a part of the institution of the Covenant People is indispensable to its existence. By the office of Moses, the Levites, and the Aaronic priesthood, God arranges that his own will and nature be the central reality of the Old Testament Church, not the people themselves. For the New Testament Church, Jesus Christ has assumed and fulfilled all forms of the offices of authority and mediation. The historical reality and meaning of the Incarnate Lord is the supreme authority whose will cannot be subverted by the self-will of the Church, however often it may be tempted to set up its own authorities. Nor can the Church, by a false understanding of "the priesthood of all believers," presume on the basis of its own sanctity ever to approach God, even in prayer and repentance, except through the one Mediator, whose work of representing us before the Holy God is the one hope we have of being God's people.

The Divine Sign of the Election of the Levites
(Num. 17:1-13)

The story in this chapter is a continuation of the affair of Korah in chapter 16, and a part of P's basic narrative. In spite of the death of Korah and his company when they instigated a lay rebellion against the special role of the Levites (16:1-35), the murmuring of Israel against Moses and Aaron continued (16: 41-50). Now the Lord gives a sign as an unmistakable manifestation of his choice of the Levites to be the ones who were qualified to draw near to him, that is, to be present in the holy precincts of the Tabernacle to perform the ritual acts of worship representing the whole people (vss. 5, 10).

On divine instruction, Moses collects from the head of each of the twelve tribes the rod or staff which each carried, possibly as a sign of office. The rod of Aaron made thirteen and represented the tribe of Levi, for the issue does not turn on Aaron's priority within the Levites, but on that of the Levites within Israel. The name of each tribe is written upon the leader's rod. The rods are then put within the Tabernacle before the Ark. The word "testimony," which is used in this chapter four times (vss. 4, 7, 8, 10), refers to the law written on tablets of stone and deposited within the Ark (Exod. 25:16, 21; 31:18). The insistence on this theme may indicate that the sign to be given was to be taken as a very ordinance of God, an implementation of the testimony.

After one night had passed, the rod with Aaron's name is found to have passed through a full year's cycle of growth; it has not only sprouted but also produced ripe almonds. This rod, miraculously changed, is put back before the Ark to remain there as a sign, a visible manifestation of God's own purpose. It shows that the special place of the Levites within Israel is God's will and is meant to prevent any further rebellion such as that of Korah (vs. 10). (On the theology of P concerning the office of the Levites, see the comment on Numbers 1:47-54; chs. 3-4; 8:5-26; ch. 18.)

Verses 12-13 form a conclusion to the Korah incident and an introduction to the instructions concerning Levites and priests in chapter 18. In this terrified, tormented lament, the people finally recognize that their holiness as the People of the Lord does not eliminate the boundary between them and God. He who is in their midst is yet wholly Other; to approach him directly without a mediator is to invite death. How then is Israel to arrange for the worship of God without profaning his holiness? This is the question to which chapter 18 is the answer.

The Work and Wages of Priests and Levites
(Num. 18:1-32)

The story of Korah's rebellion (ch. 16) and the miracle of Aaron's rod (ch. 17) dramatically made the point of the pre-eminence of the Aaronic priesthood and its unique eligibility to be present within the holy space of the Tabernacle. Israel sees that all who draw near to the Holy are in danger, and chapter 17 ends with the cry, "Are we all to perish?" Chapter 18 answers the question with a detailed description of the duties of the priests and Levites, who are to draw near to the Holy as the representatives of Israel, and therefore are to be supported by a share in Israel's offerings and tithes. Many of the matters mentioned here have already been dealt with in Leviticus 1-7 and Numbers 1-4, 8.

The duties of the priests and Levites are summarized in verses 1-7. The Levites serve and assist the priests; they may come within the Tabernacle but are not to draw near to the holy vessels or altar, which the priest alone touches. Priests and Levites are set aside and consecrated to tend the holy sanctuary, so that God's wrath may not come upon Israel because profane persons draw near the holy things of the sanctuary. The priesthood is given of God that he may be worshiped and yet reverenced in his holiness.

In verses 8-20 there is a precise list of the perquisites of the priests, including all those portions of offerings not burnt on the altar or returned to the worshiper. These the priest received for his support. The theological interpretation of this right of the priest is given in verse 20. Aaron received no inheritance in the Land of Promise when it was divided; God alone was his portion, so what was given to God by offering was shared by the priests.

In verses 21-24 the same principle is applied to the support of the Levites, for they are the possession of the Lord in redemption of all the first-born in Israel (Num. 8:14-19). The Levites receive no inheritance, but are given the tithe of all the agricultural produce which Israel brings to the Lord (Lev. 27:30-33). Verses 25-32 require that the Levites offer a tenth of Israel's tithe to God, as their own tithe to be used in support of the priests.

The axiom undergirding all these specifications is the belief that those kept from earning their own livelihood by reason of their consecration to sacred duties are to be maintained by use of part of the offerings brought to God.

Purification for Those Who Touch the Dead (Num. 19:1-22)

This chapter describes first (vss. 1-10), the way in which a special water—for purifying those who are unclean by reason of contact with the body of a dead person—is to be prepared from the ashes left from the ritual burning of a red heifer, and second (vss. 11-22), the ritual use of the water and the conditions under which death makes unclean. The chapter has closest affiliations with the laws of purification (see Lev. 11-15, and the discussion of clean and unclean there). Why it is placed in its present location in Numbers must go unanswered. That contact with the dead makes unclean is discussed at several other places in the Pentateuch (for example, Lev. 5:2; 11:24-28; 21:1-4, 10-11; 22:4-7; Num. 6:6-12). But in none of the other passages is the particular ritual of the red heifer mentioned. Although the present form of the passage presupposes the Priestly narrative, the ritual itself is obviously an ancient and primitive one—probably like the "goat for Azazel" ceremony (Lev. 16)—which was absorbed into the Israelite cult.

In Hebrews this rite for the purification of the flesh is used as an analogy to the cleansing effect of Christ's death, to show the greater and more complete value of that death to purify the conscience (Heb. 9:13-14).

The Sin of Moses at Meribah (Num. 20:1-13)

The story of the waters of Meribah tells of yet another time when Israel, faced with the hardships of the wilderness, turns on her leaders and questions her mission. But what is of special concern in this story is that the failure of faith reaches even to Moses himself, and as a result he and Aaron join the generation of those who will not enter the Promised Land. The passage is in the large from P's basic narrative; it presupposes the story of Aaron's rod (compare verse 9 with 17:10). There are touches of JE, however, in verse 1 (references to Kadesh and Miriam) and in verse 5 (it is a parallel to verse 4). In Exodus 17:1-7 there is another story of Moses bringing forth water from a rock, which is named Meribah at the end; it seems to be the counterpart in E for the present story.

According to verse 1 the people now arrive at the wilderness of Zin, the area to the north of the wilderness of Paran, where P's narrative seems to place the most of the forty-year sojourn in the wilderness. The text does not say in what year "the first month" fell, but judging from 33:36-39 it must have been the fortieth year. The JE tradition, on the other hand, located the sojourn in the Kadesh area, for it was reached in that narrative in 13:26. The death of Miriam marks the beginning of the end of the wilderness period; the first of the triumvirate which led Israel out of Egypt disappears from the scene; Aaron is soon to follow (20:22-29).

The lack of water incites the people to another rebellion against their leaders. As has become their custom in these uprisings, they heap the entire responsibility for their predicament on Moses' shoulders, say they wish they were dead, and lamentingly ask why they ever came from Egypt to the hard, barren wilderness (vss. 2-5; compare 11:1; 11:4-6; 14:2-3; 16:13-14). They speak as though their deliverance from Egypt and their pilgrimage through the wilderness were due to some crafty plan of Moses; in their self-concern over hardship they no longer can see the enterprise with the eyes of faith as the work of the Lord. Moses and Aaron turn from the mob to the Lord, going to the Tent of Meeting and falling on their faces. Knowing in faith that this people is in the hands of the Lord, they bear to him both the rebellion and the need of Israel. This time the Lord does not respond in wrath, perhaps recognizing behind the restless rebellion of Israel a desperate need. He instructs Moses to take *the* rod (vs. 8), which must refer to the rod of Aaron which had been used in the test recorded in chapter 17 and had been placed within the Tabernacle. *The* rock (vs. 8) can only be the massive hill of solid rock from beneath which the large spring of Kadesh still issues. Moses is to assemble the congregation at the rock and, as they look on, tell the rock to yield its water. The intention of so arranging things is that the water should be more than mere drink to slake Israel's thirst; as their eyes saw the Lord's provision for their need, the water would also revive their fainting faith. In I Corinthians 10:4 Paul emphasizes this point. For him the rock represents Christ, and the water is the spiritual gift which God supplies through his Son for his people in their journey through life.

What happens next (vss. 10-12) must remain to some degree an enigma, for the text does not make clear beyond any ambiguity *how* Moses failed. But verse 12 puts very clearly the *nature* and *meaning* of his failure: Moses and Aaron did not stand firm in the Lord, trusting in his power and goodness and giving themselves up to his will in such a way as to show reverence for him as God. The act of bringing forth water was meant to hallow the name of God and be a testimony to the people, but it was not done so. Actually the precise instructions of the Lord were not carried out. Instead of speaking to the rock, Moses struck it twice. This would seem a small disobedience, but the substitution of one symbolic act for another was of serious consequence in Israel's world; it changed the very character of the action. Instead of pronouncing the word of the Lord over the rock, Moses struck it, placing his own power upon it, as magicians of the time would do. The people did not *hear* the word of God, but *saw Moses* strike the rock. Moreover, the question which Moses flings at Israel in verse 10 discloses something of his inner feeling and attitude. He calls the people "you rebels"; certainly he was justified, but he rails in anger at sinners whom God will now help in mercy. And he asks, "Shall *we* bring forth water for *you?*" Notice—not "the *Lord* will," but "shall *we?*" The question is full of angry resentment. The people had turned on Moses and Aaron so many times, and now in the very face of their petulant complaining, without their having so much as a rebuke from the Lord, he was to help the rebels. On this occasion the frustration and anger of Moses matched that of the people. Psalm 106:32-33 says that Israel angered Moses and made his spirit bitter so that he spoke rash words and it went ill with Moses on their account. Numbers 20:24 and 27:14 say that Moses and Aaron rebelled against the command of God; Deuteronomy 32:51 says Moses broke faith with God and did not revere him as holy before Israel. (All these are from P. The writer of Deuteronomy, in 1:37; 3:26; 4:21, says that God was angry at Moses on account of Israel's sin; that is, Moses bore the consequences of Israel's evil himself in not being allowed to enter the Promised Land.) Moses, who so long in meekness, patience, and trust had suffered with the people whom he led, finally is shaken by their persistent faithlessness and rebellion. This one time he failed to be the man of faith; and so infinitely crucial is the responsibility of the leader for the faith of his people that Moses is not to be allowed to lead Israel into the Promised Land. Aaron, who is associated with him in this failure, is to suffer the same punishment.

In verse 13 the waters are given the name Meribah, which in Hebrew means "contention" or "striving." There is also a hint of the name "Kadesh" in the Hebrew word behind "showed himself holy." In Numbers 27:14; Deuteronomy 32:51; and Ezekiel 47: 19; 48:28 the name of this site is given as Meribath-kadesh ("Meribah of Kadesh").

Edom Refuses Passage Through Her Land
(Num. 20:14-21)

In this passage from the JE narrative, Israel makes the first move to break the generation-long camp at Kadesh in order to begin her trek around the eastern side of the Dead Sea. A glance at a map in a biblical atlas will show that the easiest route to Israel's objective in the Jordan Valley lay through the kingdoms of Edom and Moab. In ancient times there was a well-established military and trade route running north from Ezion-geber on the Gulf of Aqabah through Edom and Moab. It was Moses' intention to cross the Arabah to this "King's Highway" and to proceed north on it (vs. 17).

Edom and Moab were nations which had emerged in the thirteenth century B.C. and had established themselves as small kingdoms in the hitherto unsettled territory to the east of the Arabah and the Dead Sea. Moses had reason to expect a hospitable reception for the messengers which he sent to Edom. He refers to Israel as the "brother" of Edom (vs. 14). According to consistent biblical tradition, Edom and Israel were of the same ethnic stock (Deut. 2:4; 23:7; Obad. vss. 8-10, 12; Amos 1:11), and had derived from the same racial migrations into the Canaanite area. In the patriarchal stories Jacob, the father of Israel, and Esau, the father of Edom, were brothers (Gen. 25:19-26; 33:1-11, 15-17).

So Moses appeals to these kinsmen by reviewing, almost in confessional form, the hardships of Egypt and the deliverance of the Lord. By God's hand Israel is at Kadesh. They want only the right to passage and have no designs on Edom's territory or her

water, so precious in semi-arid regions. They will even pay the
royal toll for water rights and stay carefully on the highways, so
as not to damage fields and vineyards. But those were precarious
times, when every small nation was threatened by the pressure of
landless nomads constantly crowding their borders in endless
quest for water and arable soil. Edom's suspicions outweighed her
sympathy and sense of kinship. The king hastily marched his
army to his borders and barred Israel's passage. Moses did not
choose to contest Edom's decision, and Israel turned away to
seek another route toward her destination.

The Death of Aaron (Num. 20:22-29)

According to the basic narrative of P, to which this passage
belongs, Israel's first camp on leaving Kadesh is at Mount Hor,
where Aaron dies. The story of his death has two themes: his
death as the execution of the Lord's verdict in 20:12, and the
transfer of his priesthood to Eleazar. The location of Mount Hor
is uncertain. According to a tradition as old as the historian
Josephus, the mount was near Petra, but since Petra was within
Edomite territory that seems unlikely. Some modern geographers
place it to the northeast of Kadesh, on the west of the Arabah.
Deuteronomy 10:6 gives another name, Moserah, for the place
of Aaron's death.

Since Miriam had already died at Kadesh (20:1), Aaron is the
second of the wilderness triumvirate to pass from the scene. The
expression to be "gathered to his people [kinsmen]" is one of
the common Semitic idioms for death; the dead man is laid with
his kinsmen in the common tribal burial place and joins them in
the realm of the dead. Aaron's demise is not a normal one, by
reason of age or disease (although 33:39 gives his age as one
hundred and twenty-three years); it is the result of the Lord's
verdict upon Moses and Aaron because they rebelled against his
command at Meribah (see the comment on 20:10-12). The first
high priest himself is subject to the judgment of God, as any
man. There is nothing in him which makes him impervious to sin
or exempt from God's wrath against it. Having come to share the
failure of the wilderness generation, he too is forbidden the
Promised Land. Aaron's death is arranged as a solemn, gentle
ritual. Flanked by Moses and Eleazar, Aaron climbs Mount Hor
as the congregation watches, beholding in his quiet submission

both the willingness of faith to be in God's hand and the awful seriousness of rebellion. On the mountaintop Moses removes from Aaron the priestly garments which were the symbolic regalia of his office (Lev. 8:7-9; Exod. 28), and puts them on Eleazar, in ceremony transferring the priesthood from father to son. Then the account reports quite simply that "Aaron died there on the top of the mountain." The manner of his death is hidden in the mystery of God.

Eleazar was the third son of Aaron; the death of his elder brothers, Nadab and Abihu, is reported in Leviticus 10. In Numbers 3:32 he was appointed as leader of the Levites. He held office during the rest of Moses' life and that of Joshua. His burial on Mount Ephraim is reported in Joshua 24:33. The transfer of office from father to son is the narrative portrayal of P's belief that the priesthood was hereditary in the house of Aaron.

Victory Over Arad (Num. 21:1-3)

In the present arrangement of the material this brief story from the J narrative reports Israel's first victory over the inhabitants of Canaan. The story assumes that Israel was on the way to the north by the way of "Atharim" (the meaning of the word is unknown). Israel comes into the territory of the king of Arad, is attacked by him, and some Israelites are captured. Thereupon Israel swears a sacred oath to put the "cities" (of Arad? or the Canaanites? vss. 2-3) under the ban ("utterly destroy") if God will give them the victory. The "ban" was a practice of military operations among peoples of that time which was carried out as a sacred proceeding. A people in a city was recognized as the enemy of God and devoted or dedicated to him, the victors retaining no spoil or captives, to show that the conquest was by divine power. The practice of putting their enemies under the ban was a frequent feature of Israel's warfare in the earlier period (for example, Joshua 6:17-21; 8:24-26; Judges 20:48; 21:10-11). This savage custom seems completely reprehensible to us, however much we are ready to justify atomic warfare when it appears expedient for national interest. But if one grants as real God's involvement in human affairs through the election of Israel, there is no drawing back from the scandal of the importance of war in Israel's religious history. Israel could not have survived or played her role in "holy history" apart from a struggle with the real historical powers which threatened her emergence and existence. Israel in her military struggles as the People of God could not help seeing them from the perspective of faith.

The story as it stands is fraught with historical questions which must go without any completely satisfying solution. The traditions about Israel's route at this point all reckon with a movement around the east side of the Dead Sea; this story is set to the north of Kadesh, well up in the Negeb. The place of the battle is given the name "Hormah," which is a play on the Hebrew word for "ban" or "destruction." Hormah was given in 14:45 as the place of Israel's defeat by the Canaanites. Judges 1:16-17 says that Judah, Simeon, and the Kenites conquered a place named Zephath and changed its name to Hormah. Joshua 12:14 lists a king of Hormah and a king of Arad among those whom Joshua defeated. The relations between all these traditions and this passage have not been settled. It may be that some groups, later assimilated into the main body of Israel after the conquest, did enter from the south and gain their own territory in lower Judah.

The Fiery Serpents (Num. 21:4-9)

This is the last of the "murmuring" stories which make up the body of that part of Numbers concerned with the forty years in the wilderness. Except for the reference to the departure from Mount Hor (vs. 4a) which continues the story of Aaron's death (20:22-29) and which is from P, the story belongs to the JE narrative. Verse 4 implies that Israel had now started south in the Arabah ("way to the Red Sea") to pass around Edom's southern and eastern borders.

Because the way was long and hard the people became impatient. The Hebrew for "impatient" means literally "short of soul." The vitality of their faith ebbed as their strength was taxed. So in the final stage of their journey the people continue their pattern of complaint with incorrigible persistence. They turn the very confession of faith into doubting lamentation. When Israel recited the outline of her faith she was supposed to say, "The LORD brought us out of Egypt with a mighty hand . . . and gave us this land" (see Deut. 6:20-25; 26:5-9). But instead these people say, "Why have you brought us up out of Egypt . . .?" In their despair they exaggerate and falsify their situation; they complain to God who gives them water (20:10-13) that there is none, and to God who feeds them that they have no food. The "worthless food" which they claim to loathe is the manna (11:6-9); so they despise God's simple provision for their daily bread. On the way of life they fear death; in the presence of divine food they hunger. When faith wavers, all of God's provisions seem inadequate; and anxiety about food and clothes replaces the seeking for the Kingdom of God (Matt. 6:25-33).

In answer to the thankless blasphemy of the people, the Lord sends fiery serpents whose bite brings real death and thus shocks the people into remembering that it is life and not death that God provides for them. The punishment is calculated to drive the people to the very confession they now make. Instead of lamenting their hardships they bewail their sins—and turn for intercession to the man whom they rejected, and for help to the God whom they disdained. Such is the positive redemptive purpose of God's judgment.

The serpents are not removed, but a "salvation" is provided. The threat of death remains, lest the people again suppose they can disdain God; but a way of life which is available only to faith is provided. God instructs Moses to make a bronze serpent, an image of the real ones, to which the people who are bitten may look, and live. This arrangement seems dangerously near a kind of magic, with a charm provided which has a power independently to heal. But here the visible object is a symbol of God's word; it represents to the eye of man God's offer of help. The bronze serpent is properly interpreted in the apocryphal book, the Wisdom of Solomon (16:6-7), which calls it a "token of deliverance," and says:

> For he who turned toward it was saved, not by what he saw, but by thee, the Savior of all.

In John 3:14 Jesus uses the lifting up of the serpent in the wilderness as a type of his own availability to faith as God's provision of eternal life. In both cases the punishment for sin is the instrument for its healing. Men who look in faith behold in the Cross simultaneously the reality of their sin and the means of their redemption from it.

The record of the destruction of the bronze serpent appears in II Kings 18:4 and raises some interesting questions about its background in the religious world of early Israel's times. The image was destroyed by Hezekiah during his reformation, because the people were sacrificing to the image and calling upon it as though it were a deity. This has led some to think that the bronze serpent was a Canaanite cultic object, which had been introduced into Israel's worship, and that the story here arose to disassociate the image from its pagan meaning, and to give it a new significance in terms of Israel's own religion. Others, however, are convinced that the image does come from Moses' day and is to be identified with the "rod of God" which Moses and Aaron carried (see the serpent connections of the rod in Exodus 4:2-4; 7:10-12). The serpent was used in ancient Near Eastern religion as a divine symbol of fertility and healing by the power of pagan gods. It may be that the introduction of the serpent image into the Mosaic religion was a way to demythologize the serpent and make it merely a symbol of the Lord's power in history and in the life of his people.

The Route Around Edom and Moab (Num. 21:10-20)

Except for 10-11, these verses come from JE and give their tradition about Israel's route from the Arabah to the Jordan Valley. Verses 10-11 are written in the style of P's itinerary in chapter 33 (see vss. 43-44), and may have been placed here to harmonize the description of the two routes. Verse 4 (JE) indicates that Israel had entered the Arabah with the purpose of going around Edom; this itinerary in its present form seems to trace a route to the southern end of the Dead Sea and then east along the Brook Zered, the boundary between Edom and Moab. The location of Oboth is uncertain; most geographers place it on the west side of the Arabah. Iye-abarim ("the ruins on the other side," that is, east of the Jordan-Dead Sea line) is placed by the text to the east of Moab, and we have no indication here as to the precise route by which Israel crossed the Edom-Moab territory; it is reasonable to think that they did go along the valley of Zered.

From verse 12 on, all the mentioned sites, so far as their location is known today, are on the east side of the Dead Sea. The Arnon flows into the Dead Sea about midway on its eastern shore and is the northern boundary of Moab. Nahaliel is a valley some fifteen miles farther north. Pisgah is one of the peaks overlooking the broad plain in the valley of the Jordan, just where the river empties into the Dead Sea. The other sites mentioned are not to be located with certainty. The effect of this itinerary is to move Israel from the area of the forty-years' sojourn in the wilderness to the camp in the plains of Moab where the next series of events recorded in Numbers is to occur.

In verses 14-15, a snatch of poetry is quoted to verify the statement that the River Arnon is the northern border of Moab. The poetic fragment comes from "the Book of the Wars of the LORD," mentioned only here. The title indicates that it was a collection of stories about the battles of Israel's earliest history, when Israel fought her enemies under the inspiration and by the help of the Lord. The reference to it is a clue to the existence of literary collections of Israel's early traditions, used by the writers of the Bible but no longer extant. (See also "the Book of Jashar" in Joshua 10:13 and II Samuel 1:18.) Waheb and Suphah are names of places no longer identifiable; Ar may refer to the city of Moab, located by many on the upper reaches of the Arnon.

In verses 17-18 there is another poetic fragment, this time a refrain from a "song for the well." "Beer" (vs. 16) means "well" in Hebrew, and the place is another where God gives water to Israel (see 20:2-13; Exod. 17:1-7). The connection between God's gift of the water and the poem's statement that the well was dug by the leaders of the people is obscure.

Victory Over Sihon and Og (Num. 21:21-35)

As soon as Israel crossed the Arnon, she was in the territory of the Amorite king, Sihon. The Amorites were northwest Semitic peoples who had infiltrated the area of Canaan early in the second millennium B.C. Israel's own ancestors had been a part of this migration. But it was only in the thirteenth century that the kingdom of Sihon had emerged, through the consolidation of the territory east of the Jordan and south of the Jabbok. According to the poem in verses 27-30, Sihon had expanded his territory southward to the Arnon at the expense of Moab. His capital city was Heshbon. Though an earlier victory over the inhabitants of Canaan was reported in 21:1-3, it is in this encounter with Sihon that the JE narrative begins the story of the Conquest. Here is gained the first territory in which part of Israel will live; Sihon's land is approximately that to be settled by Reuben and Gad.

The itinerary in verses 10-20 had carried Israel to the Jordan plain; here the narrative moves back to the Arnon to tell how

Israel won her way to that point. Israel sends a message to Sihon like the one which had been dispatched earlier to Edom (20:14-21); she wants only to pass through on the King's Highway (20:17) and will not damage fields or vineyards, nor use up the water supply. Sihon's answer is the same as Edom's—he cannot risk letting Israel within his borders; and, marshaling his army, he confronts Israel at Jahaz, a site possibly located some ten miles south of Heshbon. Israel had no choice but to fight; there was no way around Sihon's territory to her destination. According to Deuteronomy 2:24-37 (a parallel account of this incident), God hardened the heart of Sihon so that Israel might defeat him and win his territory; thus, a theological interpretation of the victory is given, and the war with Sihon becomes explicitly part of God's purpose to give Israel the Promised Land. Israel wins the victory, slays Sihon, and settles his territory.

In verses 27-30 an ancient ballad is cited, ostensibly to substantiate the remark in verse 26 that Sihon had gained much of his territory from Moab. The ballad may also serve the purpose of magnifying the victory of Israel, by celebrating the prowess of the nation whom they defeated.

Verse 32 adds a brief note on the conquest of further Amorite territory in the same region. The exact location of Jazer is not known.

Verses 32-35 deal with a second campaign on the east side of the Jordan, farther to the north. The passage appears almost verbatim in Deuteronomy 3:1-3. Bashan is a fertile and well-watered region to the north of the River Yarmuk and east of the Sea of Galilee. At Israel's approach Og assembled his whole people and met them at Edre-i, one of Bashan's chief cities on the headwaters of the Yarmuk. God assures Moses that, in spite of the odds against them, Israel will win the territory. Although the exact term for the "ban" is not used (see comment on 21:1-3), the procedure is followed; all of Og's people are slain and Israel takes over his land.

Because the battles with Sihon and Og were the very first engagements by which Israel gained territory and began to realize the fulfillment of the promise to the fathers, these victories were remembered and celebrated in the recitation of the mighty acts of God (Ps. 135:11) and as an evidence of God's Covenant devotion to his people (Ps. 136:19-22).

THE CAMP IN THE PLAINS OF MOAB: PREPARATION FOR ENTERING THE PROMISED LAND

Numbers 22:1—36:13

Between Egypt and Canaan, Israel made three semipermanent encampments. The camps were at Sinai, around Kadesh, and the final one in the plains of Moab. The narrative of this part of Numbers tells about the events of the last camp before the crossing of the Jordan and in this setting places various materials which deal with Israel's settlement of Canaan. In one way or another the stories and laws brought together here prepare Israel for the occupation of the Promised Land.

The long opening sequence about the seer, Balaam (chs. 22-24), reaches its climax in his visions of the glorious future which lies ahead for Israel because God is with her. The account of Israel's apostasy in the affair of Baal of Peor (ch. 25) is a prelude to things to come when Israel enters Canaan, and a dire warning of the consequence of turning away to the gods of the land. In a second census (ch. 26) Israel is reorganized after the passing of the older generation in the wilderness. Arrangement is made for a successor to Moses in the ordination of Joshua (27:12-23). A number of units are concerned with the disposition of the land among the tribes and the principles for settling problems of possession: the two sections on the daughters of Zelophehad (27:1-11 and ch. 36), the assignment of the Transjordan territory (ch. 32), the instructions for the conquest (33:50-56), the borders of the Promised Land (ch. 34), and the selection of cities of refuge and cities for the Levites (ch. 35). The war with Midian (ch. 31) settles a matter raised in the Balaam incident. The record of Israel's itinerary (ch. 33) summarizes her journeyings. The instructions for offerings during the year (chs. 28-29) and on vows made by women (ch. 30) represent the inevitable exceptions of material for whose location no apparent reason can be discerned.

Except for the Balaam story (chs. 22-24) and the first part of the account of apostasy at Shittim (25:1-5), which are from JE, the material in this section is furnished by P. It represents the final section of the Priestly history of Israel at the time of the

normative, pre-Canaan existence. It lacks for completion only the
story of the death of Moses, which appears at the end of Deuteronomy (Deut. 34).

The effect of the whole is to show that Israel enters and settles
Canaan, not as a wave of disorganized land-hungry nomads, but
as the disciplined People of the Lord, under his instruction and
fulfilling his will. These chapters cast over the coming conquest
the aura of a ritual whose execution is fundamentally not military
or political, but religious.

Balaam and His Oracles Concerning Israel
(Num. 22:1—24:25)

The story of Balaam is the longest and most dramatic sequence
in Numbers. While Israel is camped in the plains of Moab, Balak,
the king of Moab, fearing that Israel would overwhelm him, sends
for one, Balaam, to oppose Israel with the power of a curse. But
instead of cursing, Balaam blesses Israel; he delivers four major
oracles in which he foretells the greatness and victory which are
Israel's destiny. In the architecture of the Pentateuch the Balaam
story at the close of Israel's journey is the counterpart of Pharaoh's efforts by magic and force to prevent Israel's departure at
the Exodus. The sequence bears massive testimony to the hidden
power of God's purpose at work in Israel's history, which the
powers of this world oppose in vain. The theme of the sequence
appears in the counterpoint of blessing and cursing (22:6, 12;
23:20; 24:9); the specific motif of the Abrahamic promise (Gen.
12:1-3) punctuates the entire narrative to show that God's promise to the patriarch is here being inexorably fulfilled.

Chapter 22 introduces the major characters and sets the scene.
Chapters 23 and 24 contain Balaam's four major oracles. The
first three are preceded by a ritual preparation of sacrifice, while
the fourth is delivered immediately after the third. The narratives
introducing each oracle and the oracles themselves appear in the
text as follows: (1) 22:41—23:12, with Oracle I in verses 7-
10; (2) 23:13-26, with Oracle II in verses 18-24; (3) 23:27—
24:9, with Oracle III in verses 3-9; (4) 24:10-19, with Oracle
IV in verses 15-19. There are three fragmentary oracles against
the Amalekites, Kenites, and Asshur and Eber (?) in 24:20-24.

The narrative material in these chapters comes from J and E.
Chapter 22 especially shows signs of the presence of two separate

stories which have been skillfully merged; for example, the emissaries of Balak are called both "elders" and "princes" (22:7-8). There is a particular difficulty with the part of the story about Balaam and his ass (22:21-35), because in it Balaam appears to be on his way to Moab without God's consent (verses 32-34) when he had previously been given permission to go (22:20). The inconsistency probably derives from the fact that one of the sources lets the divine permission come while Balaam is on the way, while the other tells of God's permission before he leaves. The four oracles in chapters 23-24 are among the oldest poetry in the Bible. What can be discerned about their historical environment from their content indicates that they fit very well into the conditions of the thirteenth century B.C. There is no overwhelming reason for not assigning them to Balaam in the time of Israel's conquest of the Transjordan territory.

The Coming of Balaam (22:1-40)

In 22:1-40 Balak sends for Balaam, who at his coming is already brought under the power of God. Israel's victories over the Amorites to the north of Moab (21:21-31) have caused panic among the Moabites. With Israel camped on their borders they fear a like fate for themselves. Balak makes an alliance with the Midianites, a nomadic people who roam the wilderness to the east and south of Moab, and proposes a devilish scheme to weaken the power of Israel so that the allies can drive them from the region. They will employ Balaam to curse Israel.

The figure of Balaam is something of an enigma, for the text of these chapters does not answer unambiguously all the questions we naturally raise about him. What was Balaam, that Balak should seek his assistance against Israel? All the descriptions of him, here and elsewhere in the Bible, indicate that Balaam was a professional diviner or seer, that is, a man who sought to learn the will of the gods by the observation and the interpretation of omens, or by seeking a vision in a self-induced hypnotic trance, or through dreams. Balak's messengers had to wait overnight for Balaam to receive a revelation, which seems to have been given in a dream (22:8-13, 19-21). In the oracles Balaam describes himself as seeing visions while falling down (in a trance) with eyes uncovered (24:3-4, 15-16). Joshua 13:22 calls him a "soothsayer" (diviner); the elders of Moab carry him fees for divination (22:7); before speaking his oracles he goes apart "to

look for omens" (24:1). Ancient people believed that the words
of such a man carried a power which came from the divinity
which revealed them; the words had the capacity to cause to
happen whatever they said. If the words were evil, then misfortune would ensue; but if good, then fortune would follow. Apparently Balaam had an extraordinary reputation as a practi-
tioner in the art of blessing and cursing (22:6). Balak's plot is
clear. He would oppose Israel with the dark, fearsome power of
the curse. The contest would not be one simply between men of
flesh and blood, but divine powers would be set in operation
against the Covenant People. Because this is so, the Balaam story
is crucial and climactic in the history of God's people. In the
arena created by Balaam's plot, it was not just historical nations
that were in conflict. The spiritual power of ancient paganism is
aligned against the power of the Lord, and the outcome will be a
testimony to the supremacy of the God of Sinai over the demonic
powers as well as over history.

Where was Balaam from? According to 22:5 he lived "at
Pethor, which is near the River [the Euphrates], in the land of
Amaw." Assyrian inscriptions mention a site, Petru, south of
Carchemish which is thought by many to be the same as Pethor.
In 23:7 Balaam says he comes from "the eastern mountains," that
is, the Anti-Lebanon and contiguous regions to the east of northern Phoenicia. All this indicates a home in Mesopotamia, some
400 miles distant to the north from Moab (see also Deut. 23:4).
In this case, the messengers of Balak, in their two round trips
to Pethor, would have been involved in a trip which lasted for
months. Instead of "the land of Amaw," the Hebrew text has
rather "the land of his people" (that is, his homeland). Several
of the ancient versions of the Old Testament have, instead of
"his people," the name "Ammon." There was Ammonite territory
just to the east of Edom, an easy trip by donkey (note 22:21). In
a later story, Balaam is connected with Midian (31:8, 16). What
this ambiguous evidence all means is not clear. Perhaps Balaam
was from Mesopotamia but was practicing his profession in the
Ammonite area, and the two literary sources preserved both traditions.

There is a difficult question concerning Balaam's relationship
to the Lord, the God of Israel. In the present story Balaam is
clearly not a member of the Covenant People; he is an outsider,
practicing a profession forbidden in Israel, called in to oppose

God's destiny for Israel. Yet, the deity who speaks to Balaam is from the first "the LORD" (the proper name of Israel's Covenant God), and in 22:18 Balaam refers to "the LORD my God." Did Balaam know of the Covenant God of Israel? The possibilities are too complicated for discussion here. It seems most likely that the relation of Balaam to the God of Israel is an interpretative motif. The Israelite narrator sees that, from the first, Israel's God is indeed the power controlling Balaam and speaking through him, and so he tells the story with this insight as a constitutive part of the narrative.

In fact, it is just this point which is made by the two sequences which tell how Balaam dealt with Balak's invitation and finally came to his aid. In the first (22:7-20) Balaam refuses the initial request of Balak, because he learns from God that Israel is subject to blessing instead of a curse. But when the messengers of Moab and Midian appear again, God instructs Balaam to go, with the proviso that he do only what God bids him do. In the second sequence, the story about Balaam's ass (22:21-35), Balaam starts out with the two servants to comply with Balak's plan. But God sends his angel to be Balaam's adversary to oppose his going; Balaam's life is saved only because the ass can see the terrible messenger when Balaam cannot. Balaam offers to return home, but he is allowed to go on now that he knows he is under the power of God and can speak only the word which God gives him. In both sequences Balaam arrives in Moab already brought under the power of God whose way and purpose are being manifested in Israel's history. The modern reader is tempted to pay most attention to the marvelous fact that Balaam's ass speaks to him. This surprising fact, however, is part of the humor which infects the whole story. Balaam appears as a pompous, confident ass himself, hardly possessed of the insight of his mount. The Hebrew would have found the story uproariously funny. The ass says nothing important to the story; he merely reproaches his master with injustice. It is the angel who brings the message of God to Balaam.

The First Oracle (22:41—23:12)

The second act of the Balaam story begins at a sacred high place, probably a shrine to the god Baal of Peor (see the comment on 25:1-18). From its elevation Balaam can see the nearest part of Israel's camp in the plain below. Seven altars are prepared, on each of which is sacrificed a bull and a ram, an offering by Balak in the hope of influencing the divine powers to grant a curse on Israel. Balaam goes apart to await alone the inspiration of God, and when God has given him a message he returns to Balak and his retinue.

Like the subsequent ones, this first discourse is cast in the form of a poetic description of a vision. Balaam reports what he sees not only with his eyes but by his inspired insight. He looks down upon Israel and beholds their meaning and future. What he says is the exact opposite of Balak's desired curse; he cannot curse a people whom God has not cursed. Indeed, Israel is more than a nation of wandering nomads, one among many peoples seeking land for themselves. These people are in some strange way different and bear the consecration of God. They are marked by the loneliness of election and do not reckon themselves to be one among the nations. They are a holy nation, a kingdom of priests (Exod. 19:4-6), in whose existence the government of God is hidden. The phrase, "dust of Jacob," is undoubtedly an allusion to the promise to the fathers that their descendants would be as numerous as the dust of the earth (for example, Gen. 13:16; 28:14). Here the promise of God is already at work; its blessing cannot be turned back by any curse. Balaam is so overwhelmed that he concludes with the wish that he could become one with them in their rightness before God and in his blessing.

The Second Oracle (23:13-26)

Balak is of course dismayed; his enemies are receiving a blessing instead of a curse. Though Balaam has warned him that he can speak only what God gives him to say, Balak proposes the strategy of moving their location and repeating the entire procedure. They go to the top of Pisgah, a peak in the same region, from which not so much of Israel can be seen. Perhaps Balaam was unduly influenced by seeing the extensive camp and will do better if he can only glimpse it. Leaving Balak beside his altars, Balaam goes to receive the second vision.

This time the words of the oracle are addressed directly to Balak, in answer to his hope that the second message will be different. God does not lie or change his mind as men do. The pagan gods may be thought of as subject to the persuasion of sacrifice and incantation, but this is no more than the betraying sign that they are really human. The true God brings his purpose to pass; his word is always fulfilled. And he has not planned misfortune and trouble for Israel, but blessing. The great reality of Israel is the Covenant fact: "The LORD their God is with them." Upon this unshakable rock all the wiles of Balak will shatter. "The shout of a king" refers to the vigorous outcry of Israel's praise as they worship around the Tent of Meeting, greeting God as their King with joyous acclaim. The victory over Pharaoh at the Exodus is the testimony to God's strength, and because of him Israel is strong like the wild ox of the desert or the lion who takes prey when it will. Against a strength that belongs to God, no enchantment or divination will work.

The Third Oracle (23:27—24:9)

With Balaam continuing to protest that he can only speak what God permits, Balak once more tries the strategy of moving the place of the divination ritual. The relation of the third location, the top of Peor, to the top of Pisgah is uncertain. The ritual of the seven altars is held a third time. But Balaam, by now convinced that there is no hope of receiving a curse from God, makes no attempt to seek omens of divination. Instead he faces toward Israel's camp, surveying the tenting tribes covering the landscape; and then the Spirit of God falls upon him, bringing him to that ecstatic seizure by the personal force of God which characterized Israel's own early prophets.

This discourse is a lyric description of the beauty and strength which Balaam beholds in Israel. It is spoken, as it were, not to Balak, but to Israel. Balaam begins (vss. 3-4) by describing how the oracle comes to him as a vision in a trance. Using the loveliest comparisons, he pictures the beauty and prosperity of the Israel that is to be (vss. 5-7). He looks at Israel's camp, and before his eyes appears a vast, well-watered garden, full of aloes and cedars, a luxuriant oasis in the wilderness, in prophecy of the blessing which is to be worked out for Israel. The line, "his king shall be higher than Agag," foresees the victory of Saul over the Amalekite king in I Samuel 15 (however, the ancient versions are divided on the proper reading of the name). Verse 8 and the first two lines of verse 9 are substantially repetitions of motifs in the second oracle (23:22, 24) and celebrate the invincible strength of God who, having brought his people out of Egypt, makes them irresistible against their foes. The description reaches its climax in the pronouncement of a formula from the Abrahamic promise (Gen.

12:3; 27:29): "Blessed be every one who blesses you, and cursed
be every one who curses you." With that sentence it becomes plain
that not only does God's election keep Israel safe in his blessing,
but that those who attempt to curse Israel put themselves under
God's curse. The Chosen People create a crisis for all around
them, because God appears in their history to set up his rule. The
attitude that one assumes toward their history is decisive for one's
relationship to God's purpose to bless the whole earth through his
rule.

The Fourth Oracle (24:10-19)

Balak is beside himself with anger. His whole scheme has back-
fired. Now his enemies stand under a threefold blessing. Lest the
situation grow worse he peremptorily orders Balaam out of his
kingdom, with no reward. But Balak cannot halt a process which
he has begun. Balaam speaks yet a fourth oracle, this time without any ritual preparation. In it he foresees the doom of Moab.

In Balaam's fourth discourse he tells of a vision in which he
looks into the future to behold the appearance of a royal figure in
Israel whose dominion shall extend over all the surrounding peoples. He begins (vss. 15-16), as in the third, with a description of
how the vision comes from God while he is in a trance. And then
he tells how the curtains of the future drop away, so that he can
behold one who is yet to come (vs. 17):

> I see him, but not now;
> I behold him, but not nigh.

Balaam characterizes this mysterious figure of the future by the
terms "star" and "scepter," which obviously portray the coming
one as a king. The scepter is one of the insignia of a king. "Star"
was used in Israel and the ancient Near East as a metaphor for a
royal person (Isa. 14:12). In this king the powerful purpose of
God to reign on earth as he does in heaven will be manifested.
Moab, Sheth (the tribal name of the Sutu, mentioned in Egyptian
texts of the nineteenth century B.C.), Edom, and Seir will all be
conquered by Israel under this royal figure. The only future for
Balak and his neighbors is the future which God works out in his
way with Israel. The kingdoms of this world stand under the crisis
of the Reign of God.

After Old Testament times this prophecy was interpreted by
both Judaism and early Christianity in a Messianic sense. In the

first centuries A.D. the Jewish revolutionary Bar-Cochba was called "the Son of the Star." In Revelation 22:16 Jesus, as the descendant of David, is hailed as "the bright morning star." Within Israel's history the victories listed in the discourse fit best with the military campaigns of David. As the elect and anointed ruler of God's people, David is the first reference of the prophecy. But true prophecy always transcends its immediate reference. The faith that knows the historical fulfillment of the Messianic purpose in Jesus Christ senses in this ancient oracle a direction toward the irruption of God's Reign in his appearing. Hidden within the military and political idiom of Balaam's speech is the plan of God to win back his world and bring all people under the gentle sway exercised through the greatest Son of David.

Three Brief Concluding Oracles (24:20-25)

Immediately on finishing the fourth major discourse Balaam delivers prophecies concerning the fate of the Amalekites, the Kenites, and Asshur and Eber. These prophecies essentially continue the assertions of the fourth oracle about the future defeat of the Transjordan nations and tribes. The Amalekites were a nomadic people who ranged the desert to the south of Palestine; they were defeated by Gideon (Judges 7) and Saul (I Sam. 15) and were finally subdued by David. The Kenites were another tribe of the Sinai peninsula and the Arabian wilderness with whom Israel had many contacts in the Mosaic era. The third discourse (vss. 23-24) appears in a very difficult and corrupt text in Hebrew; it may refer to the circumstances surrounding the invasions of the sea peoples along the coast of Palestine in the thirteenth century B.C. Indeed, the historical reference and meaning of all these concluding lines is quite obscure, and at present they are among the least understood texts in the Old Testament.

Israel's Unfaithfulness at Shittim (Num. 25:1-18)

The story of Israel's unfaithfulness at Shittim is composed of two parts which differ somewhat. The first (vss. 1-5) is from JE; the second (vss. 6-18) is from P. The story is not told twice, nor are the two accounts interwoven, as is often the case. Instead, JE furnishes the beginning and P the conclusion; we have neither the end of JE's story nor the beginning of P's. In the JE section the other nation is Moab; the problem is apostasy to Baal of Peor;

and God's wrath is expressed through a verdict against the guilty, handed down by Moses. In the P section the other nation is Midian; the focus of attention is on a case of intermarriage; the priest Phinehas is the principal character; and God's wrath is expressed in the form of a plague. But P's section may well be the conclusion to its story of the same incident; the temptation through women figures in both stories, and a plague for some sin is already in progress when the P narrative commences.

Shittim (Hebrew "the Acacia"), which appears as "Abel-shittim" in 33:49, is a site opposite Jericho on the eastern edge of the Jordan Valley. It was the last station before Israel entered Palestine proper; Israel camped there for some time to consolidate her situation before pressing on across the Jordan. During the encampment some of the Israelite men began to commit fornication with Moabitish women, and under their influence became involved in the religious rituals of Moab. The sacrifices to which the Israelites were invited were sacred meals, at which the worshipers ate part of the sacrificed animal in a ritual of communion and fellowship with the deity of the throne (compare the sacrifice described in Lev. 3 and 7:11-18). The particular deity involved was the Baal of Peor. Peor is the name of a headland or peak (23:28) with a place of worship called "Beth-peor" ("Peor's House") nearby (Deut. 3:29; 4:46). "Baal" is the Canaanite word for "Lord," and is the title given to a god who was the patron deity of the place at which he was worshiped. The "Lord of Peor" may have been Chemosh, the national god of Moab.

To participate in the cult of a god was to act as a devotee of that god; in the Old Testament view there is no separating what a man is from what he does. To worship another god was a violation of the very first principle of Israel's nature as the People of the Lord (Exod. 20:3). The Covenant at Sinai committed Israel to strict and exclusive service of the Lord (Exod. 34:12-16). Here Israel, bound by the Covenant to have no other gods, becomes attached to a Moabite deity as soon as she makes camp in the territory. This infidelity was an ominous portent of things to come when Israel would settle in Canaan, with all its shrines and deities. Her very existence and the fulfillment of her role as the Chosen People depended on her will to cleave to the God of Sinai as her one true God.

The Lord in his wrath commands Moses to execute the offenders. Verse 4 implies that the chiefs of the people are punished, but the Hebrew text may mean that the chiefs were ordered to execute the guilty persons. In verse 5 the leaders, who are called "judges," are commanded to execute the men who are yoked to the Baal of Peor (the change in titles, "chiefs" to "judges," arises from the joining of J and E). The execution by hanging the men up in the sun seems to mean that the men were killed, their limbs broken, and their corpses hung up for public viewing. At the very beginning of her life as Covenant People, Israel had fallen into apostasy in the matter of the golden calf (Exod. 32); here at the culmination of her pilgrimage to the Promised Land, she is unfaithful again. The gods of this world are a constant hazard to the life of Covenant faith. The two stories of Sinai and Shittim are double witness to the first principle of biblical faith for the People of the Lord—exclusive and total devotion to the God of the Covenant.

As the P narrative takes up the story in verses 6-18, a plague is in progress, apparently as a result of Israel's apostasy in the missing part of the narrative (see vs. 18). The people are all gathered at the Tent of Meeting, "weeping" before the Lord. From this incident there developed a practice of ritual lamentation by the congregation, reflected in a number of the Psalms (Pss. 44, 74, 79, 80, 83). While the lamentation was being held, one Zimri brought a Midianite woman named Cozbi into the camp (vss. 6, 14-15). The expression "brought . . . to his family" means "took her as his bride." Thus, the focus of the story now becomes a case of intermarriage with a foreign woman who was a devotee of another god. The corruption of Israel's faith through intermarriage with pagan people was a continuous danger for Israel. The Priestly narrative manifests a constant interest in the problem (for example, Gen. 26:34-35; 28:1-2), and this story would have had a crucial relevance in the postexilic period when Ezra was struggling to turn back the tide of paganism in Judah by breaking up the marriages of Jews and non-Jews (see Ezra 10).

Phinehas, the son of Aaron's successor as chief priest, is clearly the second crucial concern of the P story. His execution of Zimri and Cozbi was not a heedless act of violence; the very life of Israel was at stake, for 24,000 had already died because of the plague provoked by just such disobedience to God's will (vs. 9). The terrible devotion of Phinehas to the purity of Israel was the occasion for staying the plague, just as the unfaithfulness of the people had caused its appearance. He entered into the very jealousy of the Lord himself for his people. "Jealousy" and "wrath" are feelings we regard as unlovely in persons. But in the nature of God they are always expressions of his will to fulfill his saving purpose and bring in his Kingdom; they describe the action of God in his very real involvement with human beings. "Jealousy" or "zeal" is the Lord's passionate caring that his people be devoted to him alone.

When Phinehas acts in identity with the zealous concern of the Lord for the purity of Israel, he shows himself a worthy instrument of God's purpose and is designated as the successor to Eleazar as chief priest. Here God's Covenant is given Phinehas as a promise, and the priesthood is assigned to his descendants in perpetuity. The genealogy in Ezra 7:1-6 puts the Zadokites among the descendants of Phinehas; so the present story may serve also to vindicate the ancient origin of the Zadokite priesthood.

Verses 16-18 are a conclusion to the two stories in their combined form. The Midianites, who were the tribe of Jethro (Exod. 3:1) and Hobab (Num. 10:29), became the object of dedicated hostility, this probably in anticipation of the war with Midian in chapter 31. Numbers 31:16 states that Balaam had cunningly put the Midianite women up to the seduction of the Israelites to provoke the wrath of the Lord against Israel; verse 18 seems to reflect this tradition also. It may have been in the lost part of the P narrative, but Balaam's story in chapters 22-24, of course, has nothing of this.

The Second Census (Num. 26:1-65)

The preparation for leaving Sinai to begin the pilgrimage to the Promised Land was opened with a census (Num. 1). A second numbering of Israel concludes the wilderness wandering and marks a second phase of preparation for the conquest of Canaan. It was commanded by the Lord "after the plague" (vs. 1); the period of chastisement for the failure in the wilderness was over, and all the generation of Hormah (14:26-45) were dead save Joshua and Caleb. It was time to regroup the forces of Israel for the campaign which lay ahead. In this second census the motif of preparation for the division of the Promised Land is added (vss. 52-56). Israel stands on the threshold of the inheritance of the land in fulfillment of the promise to the fathers.

The second census of the twelve tribes is conducted much as

was the first. (See the comment on Numbers 1 for its military character and the difficulty with the totals given for the number of Israelites.) The males in each of the twelve tribes (counting Manasseh and Ephraim as two) were numbered. A separate census was held for the tribe of Levi (compare Num. 3). The total for the twelve tribes came to 601,730, less than the number of the first census. (If one reckons by the system outlined in the comment on Numbers 1, the total is 596 units of fighting men, adding up to 5,750 in all.)

The Daughters of Zelophehad (Num. 27:1-11)

The census (ch. 26) in preparation for the division of the land to the tribes and their clans raised a special problem for the daughters of Zelophehad, whose story is here told by P. Zelophehad was a Manassite who had no sons; his only children were five daughters (26:33), to whom normal Hebrew custom would not allow a father's inheritance to go. The problem was not merely the disposal of property. If the children of Zelophehad received no share of the Promised Land, they would not be included in the inheritance of the People of the Lord; the name of their father would vanish as though he had not existed. So the five daughters brought the case to Moses and Eleazar and the congregation for decision before the Lord. Moses received a decision on their case which is extended to a general law: where there are no sons, a father's inheritance passes to his daughters, next, to his brothers, or, lacking these, to the nearest kinsman.

Compared with the nations around them, Israel always sought to protect and develop the rights of women. This Priestly story, with its accompanying law, is one more step toward that Church in which there is neither male nor female as respects privilege before Christ. The request of these courageous women is vindicated by God; daughters as well as sons are to have place in the inheritance of the People of the Lord.

The names of the five daughters appear elsewhere as the names of towns and clans within Manassite territory. Tirzah was a Canaanite city to the northeast of Shechem. Noah and Hoglah are also names appearing in eighth-century inscriptions. Apparently, the Priestly narrative drew on actual traditions deriving from the division and settlement of Canaan by the tribes. A different aspect of the case comes up again in Numbers 36. In Joshua

17:3-6 the daughters are assigned their share of Manassite territory.

The Ordination of Joshua (Num. 27:12-23)

Although Moses is here instructed to prepare for his mysterious
departure from Israel, the account of his death does not appear
until the end of Deuteronomy (34:1-8), where the instructions of
Numbers 27:12-14 are repeated (Deut. 32:48-52). In the present
form of the Pentateuch, the rest of Numbers and all of Deuteronomy stand between the instructions in this passage and the account of Moses' death. It is probable that, in P's basic narrative,
Moses' death followed these first instructions. The displacement
was effected when Numbers 28-36 was added to P's basic narrative
and Deuteronomy was incorporated in the Pentateuch.

The Lord commands Moses to go up on "this mountain of
Abarim" to see the Promised Land, into which he is not to enter.
After he has viewed it in the distance, he will be "gathered to . . .
[his] people" (an expression of the Hebrew conception of death).
As punishment for his failure at Kadesh he cannot lead Israel into
Canaan (20:1-13). There he had "rebelled against . . . [the] word"
of God; he whose distinction lay in God's speaking with him
"mouth to mouth" (12:8) had not followed the word of the Lord,
and so had not sanctified him. The peak, referred to here only as
one of "the Abarim" (mountains in Transjordan), is named specifically as Mount Nebo in Deuteronomy 34:1 (P), or as Pisgah
in Deuteronomy 3:27.

With Moses' death at hand, the question about Israel's leadership became an urgent one. Moses had suffered with and for this
people, had wrestled with them in their rebellion, and had prayed
for them in their sin. He could not bear to think of them leader-
less, a flock without a shepherd. He knew them well enough to
anticipate what would become of their march into the Promised
Land. So Moses intercedes with the Lord to appoint a man to
live before them and lead them in all their corporate actions as
"the congregation." Without a man of God in their midst and at
their head, the congregation would disintegrate into scattered individuals without purpose or unity. "As sheep which have no
shepherd" is a frequently used expression for the tragic situation
of God's people when they lack a leader whose authority keeps
them in the way of the Lord (I Kings 22:17; Ezek. 34:5; Zech.

10:2; 13:7; Mark 6:34). In the New Testament, Jesus appears as the Shepherd of the sheep of Israel (John 10:11; Heb. 13:20; I Peter 2:25), and so succeeds to the office of divinely designated leader of the Covenant People, fulfilling the office held by Joshua and those who follow.

The Lord selects Joshua, the son of Nun, one of the two spies who had advocated the attack on Canaan from the south when the others had rebelled (14:4-10). Joshua is qualified, because he is "a man in whom is the spirit." "Spirit" is the endowment of a man by God with the qualities needed for an office within his people. In Joshua's case, he possesses the spirit of wisdom (Deut. 34:9). Moses is to ordain Joshua in a service attended by all the congregation and presided over by Eleazar, the priest. Moses first lays his hands on him, a ritual act still used in the ordination service of church and synagogue. And Moses is to charge Joshua concerning his duties. In this way Moses is to bestow on Joshua some of his own "authority" (the Hebrew word means the "majesty" which marks a regal leader). The ordination service is a compelling instruction to the congregation that Joshua is chosen of God. Moses' successor is not selected by fleshly descent or popular choice, but by the election of God through the instrument of the Spirit.

Though Joshua is successor to Moses, he is not his equal. Where Moses received divine instruction directly from God, Joshua is to be directed by the priest, who will learn God's will by using the sacred lot, the Urim (compare Exod. 28:30; Lev. 8:8). The Priestly tradition insists upon the pre-eminence of Moses as mediator of divine instruction, but after Moses it is the priest alone who is the locus of divine instruction for the congregation. Joshua is to lead Israel in war and peace, according to God's will mediated through the chief cultic official. The unity of Moses' office is divided between priest and military leader.

A Manual of Offerings for the Holy Year
(Num. 28:1—29:40)

The purpose of these two chapters is described in 28:2; they give a detailed list of the offerings, including animal sacrifice, cereal offerings, and drink offerings, which are to be brought to the Temple on the stated seasons of Israel's religious year. The form in which this Priestly material appears here is postexilic, though many of its elements are quite ancient. Most of the matters dealt with in these chapters have been treated earlier. (See the comment on the types of offerings and their technical terminology, in Leviticus 1-7; on the religious calendar, in Leviticus 23; on the measurement of drink and cereal offerings to be used with various animal sacrifices, in Numbers 15:1-16. For a similar and somewhat earlier list, see Ezekiel 45:18—46:15.)

Offerings are prescribed for the following times: (1) the continual burnt offering (28:3-8) brought in the morning and evening of each day so that the fire of sacrifice may burn perpetually on the altar of burnt offering; (2) the Sabbath (28:9-10); (3) the first day of each month (28:11-15); (4) the Passover (28:16), which is listed without specified offerings because it has its own peculiar ritual; (5) the Feast of Unleavened Bread (28:17-25) for all its seven days; (6) the Feast of Weeks on the day of First Fruits (28:26-31); (7) the day of blowing the trumpets or New Year's Day (29:1-6); (8) the Day of Atonement (29:7-11); (9) the Feast of Booths (29:12-38), with all of its eight days treated separately.

Laws Concerning Vows Made by Women (Num. 30:1-16)

These priestly regulations on vows are specifically concerned with protecting the rights of a husband or father, where a wife's or a daughter's vow contradicted her responsibility to him (vs. 16). (For other ordinances on vows, see Leviticus 5:4-6; ch. 27; Numbers 6; Deuteronomy 23:21-23.) A vow committed a person to some special deed or gift to God, or to some abstinence, or to a withdrawal from normal life. In verse 2 there is the general rule that every vow and pledge made by speaking must be kept. The Hebrew laid a great emphasis on speech; what is uttered becomes real and cannot be ignored, especially where a man's word binds him before the Lord.

The problem with vows made by women grew out of the possibility of their taking Nazirite vows (Num. 6:2) or interrupting conjugal relations or pledging the husband's property or making themselves ineligible for marriage. (Paul warns against excessive interruption of conjugal relations for religious reasons in I Corinthians 7:1-7.) A man is here given the right to cancel his wife's or daughter's vow by his own speech; otherwise the vow must be fulfilled. The law is concerned with the complete union of husband and wife and with actions on her part which would separate them.

None of the Pentateuchal laws require vows; they are measures to regulate their observance if one is made. Deuteronomy 23:22 states categorically that it is no sin to refrain from vows. Our Lord commands believers not to make religious vows at all (Matt. 5:33-37).

Vengeance on Midian (Num. 31:1-54)

Although Moses has been prepared for his death, he is directed by the Lord to carry out a war of vengeance on Midian (vss. 1-6). In this chapter and in 25:6-18 the Midianites seem to be thought of as a settled people, not too far distant from Israel's camp in the plains of Moab, while in the earlier traditions of Israel (Gen. 25:2, 6; Exod. 2:15) they are nomadic folk whose principal territory was in the Arabian Desert, just to the east of the Gulf of Aqabah. Israel's relationship to them in the early wilderness period was friendly and important (10:29-32).

Israel thought of the Lord as a "God of vengeance" because of his action in judgment against those who oppose his way in history (Ps. 94). The war of vengeance here described is a sequel to the divine command to harass Midian because they were the source of Israel's unfaithfulness at Shittim (vs. 16; 25:16-18). Moses prepares for the attack by drafting a thousand from each tribe. They are led, not by Joshua who was appointed in chapter 27, nor by Moses or Eleazar, but by Phinehas, who acted so resolutely in the affair of Cozbi (ch. 25). Since it is a "holy war," ordered by the Lord, Phinehas takes with him "the vessels of the sanctuary and the trumpets" as ritual symbols of the nature of the campaign. Notice that the Ark, the palladium of "holy war" in the earlier tradition, is missing.

The campaign, described briefly in verses 7-12 and only in terms of its results, is a complete success. Every Midianite man is slain. Among them are their five kings (named also in Joshua 13:21, where they are called "princes" and are associated with Sihon) and Balaam, the prophet of Numbers 22-24, who is here charged with complicity in the plot to entangle Israel in relations with the pagan god, Baal of Peor (vs. 16). The Midianite cities and camps are destroyed, their women and children captured, and their possessions plundered.

When Moses sees that the returning army has brought back the Midianite women alive he is very angry, because the war of vengeance is thereby frustrated of its purpose. It was the women, counseled by Balaam, who lured Israel into unfaithfulness (the incident is not reported in the Bible, but could have preceded the partial account of P which begins at 25:6). So Moses commands that all of them except the virgins, who obviously could not have been implicated in the plot, be put to death (vss. 13-18).

Then Moses instructs the army concerning the purification necessary before they can return to the camp (vss. 19-24). Any who touch a dead body are unclean, and they make unclean whatever they touch. So the soldiers are to purify themselves according to the ritual already specified in chapter 19. The priest Eleazar adds further instructions applying to articles which can be passed through fire or must be purified by water. These instructions are not stated elsewhere in the Old Testament.

By far the longest section of the chapter deals with the disposition of the booty (vss. 25-54). It is divided equally between the army and the congregation, according to an ancient custom of giving the camp a share in the spoils (see also I Sam. 30:22-25). Of the half assigned to the warriors, 1/500 is given to the priest as a tribute to the Lord. Of the half assigned to the congregation 1/50 is given to the Levites. The sum of the booty taken is spectacular: 32,000 virgins, 675,000 sheep, 72,000 large cattle, 61,000 asses, and jewelry worth 16,750 shekels. The jewelry is contributed by the officers to be placed in the Tent of Meeting as a memorial to the Lord, in recognition of his victory in which not one Israelite soldier was lost. It is an act similar to that of the leaders of Israel at the beginning of the wilderness march (ch. 7).

What is the purpose of this strange and, in part, brutal story of Moses and Israel? First, it must be recognized that in its present form the story is not historical. Behind it there may be a historical nucleus in Balaam's relation to Midian, which is lost with the displaced part of the P story in Numbers 25; and the J tradition does place Midian near Moabite territory (Gen. 36:35). But it is enough to remember the large part which Midian is to play at a later period in Israel's history (Judges 6-8). The Midianites were hardly exterminated before Israel entered the land. Moreover, the booty is unmanageably vast and the victory ideal—not an Israelite is lost. Second, the real interest of the story is not in the military campaign as such, but in the mere fact of vengeance on Midian, the rites of purification, and the technique for disposition of the booty. The themes of faith at work in these interests are not difficult to discern. The Lord is zealous for his way through history with Israel and acts to judge those who oppose his purpose. Israel is vigorously to maintain ritual purity as a witness to the presence of the Lord in their midst. Israel's victories are really the work of the Lord; the booty is actually his, for he commands the disposition. The story has been called an early example of a *midrash:* that is, a story which illustrates the life of faith or the proper practice of the requirements of religion. How the story developed, or how these three themes came to be united in it, one cannot say. There is evidence in the language that some older elements of historical tradition have been used. But in its present form the entire story is an addition to the basic narrative of P. The Old Testament has many accounts of war carried out at the command of the Lord as a part of the "holy history"; but this midrashic story is not the place to discuss the problems and values of Israel's tradition of "holy war." Third, the Christian must read this chapter as a Christian, interpreting in the light of Christ. He will listen for the deeper themes of faith in a vehicle whose appropriateness belongs to another time. He may be reminded here of God's involvement in the Church as a historical people, his zeal for the realization of his purpose, his concern for their purity, his demand that all glory be his.

The Assignment of the Transjordan Territory
(Num. 32:1-42)

In the cycle of stories about Israel's wilderness wanderings, early events tend to repeat themselves. In Numbers 13-14 the fearful report of the spies discouraged the people from entering Canaan from the south; now a similar disaster threatens to wreck the pilgrimage of Israel toward the inheritance which the Lord will give them. The tribes of Reuben and Gad decide that they do not want to cross the Jordan, the threshold of the Promised Land (vs. 5). Both tribes owned large herds of cattle. They had seen that the land which Israel had captured from Sihon was ideal for grazing. Faced with such an opportunity to occupy prime cattle country, they were willing to drop out of the hard and vigorous enterprise of the conquest of Canaan. The promise of prosperity loomed larger than the promise of a destiny as the People of the Lord.

Moses is appalled. He sees their proposal as a revival of Israel's earlier failure at Kadesh. If the tribes of Reuben and Gad sit out the coming war of conquest, it is sure to discourage the rest of Israel from going on in obedience to the purpose of the Lord. And then the disaster which had been averted in the earlier incident only by the insistent intercession of Moses (14:11-25) will occur. The Lord will depart from those who will not wholly follow him. He goes not with those who go not with him. The inevitable result will be the end of a people whose existence is the work of the Lord (vs. 15).

Confronted with such an interpretation of their proposal, Reuben and Gad advance an alternative plan. They will rebuild the cities in the desired territory, secure their families, flocks, and herds in them, and then accompany the other tribes in the conquest. They will not return until the whole people has gained its inheritance, and then they will accept the territory east of the Jordan as their inheritance. Moses agrees to this alternative plan. If the Reubenite and Gadite warriors participate in the Conquest they will acknowledge their commitment to the calling and mission of the people of Israel. The unity of the people is a great issue here; they are not called as tribes or individuals, but only as a people. Any defections from the mission of Israel compromised the obedience of the whole. Too, the way in which the land was to be settled was at stake. It could not be occupied merely as a military conquest, an action with only human dimensions. It had to be settled through ritual action which symbolized the fact that it was received at the hand of the Lord; it must be distributed by the leaders as inheritance. This is why Moses instructs Joshua and Eleazar to give them the land in the ritual division which is to take place later after the Conquest (Joshua 13). It is not theirs to settle; it must be given them, and they can receive it only as a part of the Israel of God.

Clear as the themes of this story are, the chapter is packed with literary and historical problems. How do Reuben and Gad happen to own more cattle than the other tribes? Is this not a result of their residence in Gilead's excellent range country, rather than its cause? The border between Reuben and Gad is usually thought of as a clear dividing line, drawn east from the north end of the Dead Sea (Joshua 13:15-28), but the cities assigned to Reuben and Gad overlap and indicate a common possession of the territory between the Jabbok and Arnon rivers. The half-tribe of Manasseh, made up of the clans of Machir, Jair, and Nobah, appear in verses 33, 39-42, without any real place in the story elsewhere. They are assigned territory to the north of the Jabbok, which they conquer independently in an operation similar to those described in Judges 1. Moreover, the literary composition of the chapter is complex, for it shows characteristics of all the major strands of the Pentateuch—JE, P, and even D. In its present form chapter 32 has been rewritten as a part of the final revision of the P history.

But whatever tentative solutions one may reach in relation to these questions, the chapter is based on the clear historical fact that Reuben, Gad, and some Manassite clans did settle in Gilead, and it asserts the theological affirmation that this geographical separateness was not a division of the unity of all Israel as responsible for her mission and as recipients of the Lord's blessing.

The Route of Israel from Egypt to the Plains of Moab (Num. 33:1-49)

With the wilderness journey behind, the route followed during the pilgrimage from Egypt to the plains of Moab is now set down in precise detail by listing in order the sites of Israel's encampments. The appearance of the itinerary here indicates that a significant chapter of Israel's history is complete. It began with the mighty acts of the Lord in Egypt—his victory over the world power of Egypt and her gods (vss. 3-4). It reaches its climax on the plains of Moab, with Israel poised for the final movement of her pilgrimage, the conquest of the Promised Land.

Beginning with Rameses, forty sites are listed on the way to the plains of Moab. The places named cover the three principal phases of Israel's journey as it is depicted in Exodus and Numbers: verses 5-15 the journey from Rameses to Sinai, verses 16-36 the route from Sinai to Kadesh, and verses 37-49 the trek around to the east of Canaan at the edge of the Jordan Valley. The journey begins on the fifteenth day of the first month of the first year. The only other calendar notice is that of Aaron's death at Mount Hor on the first day of the fifth month of the fortieth year. If the itinerary presupposes a year for the first phase (Num. 10:11) and forty years for the whole, then ten stations belong to the first year, twenty-one to the second phase, and nine to the last phase.

Some of the sites named as encampments of Israel in this chapter appear elsewhere only in JE material, and others appear only in P. Some are not mentioned outside this chapter. The number (forty) may point to an ideal itinerary accommodated to the tradition of forty years in the wilderness, though the dates clearly indicate that a stay of a year at each is not presupposed. Verse 2 attributes this record to Moses, an unusual specification of authorship; some scholars think that the final editor of the itinerary was working with a very ancient itinerary for pilgrimage to Sinai, assigned by tradition to Moses.

The precise location of some of these sites is unknown; the identification of others is only tentative. Wilderness camps do not leave lasting memorials, and often their names perish with those who used them. So the exact route here described cannot be drawn on a map with certainty. Informed proposals will be found in a good Bible atlas. The sites whose locations are sure indicate a route moving across the peninsula of Sinai (either by a swing south or straight) to Ezion-geber, then northwest to Kadesh, and finally east through Edom and north to the plains of Moab. What this itinerary with all its careful detail does demonstrate is Israel's strong faith in the reality of her history under God. It was not a phantasy, but a real historical way, involving places and distances and times. The old route of the wilderness would always have something to say about the historical way yet to be traveled.

Instructions Concerning the Conquest of Canaan (Num. 33:50-56)

This passage covers two matters which are raised because the conquest of Canaan is in immediate prospect. First, the land is to be purged of its pagan inhabitants, along with all their places and paraphernalia for worship (vss. 51-53, 55-56). Second, the land is to be divided among the tribes by lot (vs. 54). Verse 54 is clearly from the editor of P and points forward to chapter 34; the rest of the material has the characteristic expressions of H and D. The inhabitants of Canaan are to be driven out because their pagan faith would be a threat to Israel's loyalty to the Lord (vs. 55). Particularly, their use of images at their cultic centers ("high places") was in utter contradiction to the distinctive religion of Israel (vs. 52). The Canaanites' worship of false gods was the theological justification for their displacement by Israel; and if Israel fell into their ways, Israel would be treated by God as the Canaanites were treated (vs. 56).

The Extent and Division of the Promised Land
(Num. 34:1-29)

When Israel, as one people, entered the Promised Land they were to divide the land among the tribes, as the Lord directed, through the use of the sacred lot (vss. 13-14). No tribe was to claim its own land; all was to be apportioned as a gift, an inheritance from the Lord. Preparation for the ceremony of division (described in Joshua 13-17) is made before the tribes cross the Jordan to begin their conquest of Canaan.

The boundaries of Canaan are described in verses 1-15. The territory enclosed by these borders was certainly not occupied by Israel during the conquest under Joshua or in the later campaigns described in Judges. The borders would come nearest to fitting the territory conquered by David; and the lines have some affinity with the ideal portrayal of Israel's territory in Ezekiel 47 and 48. The southern boundary fits well with what is known of the tribal period (Joshua 15:1-4). The western and eastern boundaries follow the coast and the Jordan Valley, except for Reuben, Gad, and the half-tribe of Manasseh on the eastern side (vss. 13-15; see Num. 32). The northern boundary is the most unclear because most of its sites are unknown.

In verses 16-29 officials are appointed to be in charge of the division. Eleazar the priest and Joshua are to preside. The list of "leaders" from each of the twelve tribes reflects the old organization of Israel as a twelve-tribe league, probably coming from premonarchial times. Similar lists of leaders appear in Numbers 1: 5-16; 13:4-16.

The Cities of Refuge and the Levitical Cities
(Num. 35:1-34)

The Priestly narrative fuses, here as elsewhere, the arrangement for cities of refuge and that for cities in which the Levites are to dwell. In its story the plan to establish cities for the Levites, with some designated as cities of refuge, is set up by Moses as part of the advance preparation in the plains of Moab for the organization of life in Canaan. The Lord commands that the Levites, who as a tribe consecrated for service to the Tabernacle will have no portion of the land assigned to them (Num. 18:23-24), be given cities in the territory of the other tribes, with grazing rights in the immediate neighborhood. They were to have forty-eight cities in all. This provision is carried out in Joshua 21, where the cities are named in a list which gives evidence of deriving from David's time. The arrangement is undoubtedly schematized in the Priestly account, but it clearly has a historical background. After all, the Levites had to settle somewhere, and their grouping may have been defined when they were going to and from Jerusalem to serve their shifts at the Temple after Josiah's reform, and may have emerged in concentrations around cities which had their own shrines before the reform.

Of the forty-eight Levitical cities, six were to be named as cities of refuge (vs. 6), and the larger part of the chapter (vss. 9-34) is devoted to the laws which governed their use. Three were to be in Canaan and three on the east of Jordan, so that one served each region of those two sections. The cities are named and established in Joshua 20. To these cities a man who killed another without meaning to do so, or without malice aforethought (see the illustration in Deut. 19:5), could flee and then remain in custody. The elders of his city would try his case, and if he were not proved a murderer he could remain safely in the city of refuge until the death of the high priest, which brought a general amnesty. Then he was free to return to his own city. But if he was guilty of murder, or left the city, he would be executed by the "avenger of blood."

The "avenger of blood" was the nearest kinsman of the slain man. According to the ancient customs of the desert people, brought with Israel to Canaan, the shedding of blood had to be dealt with by the closest kinsman of the one who died. This was not only a matter of primitive justice; it was considered that the shed blood of a member of the tribe injured the tribe and polluted its land until the killer's blood was spilled to expiate it (vs. 33). The practice meant endless strife and many killings for vengeance which was unjustified. Early in her history Israel acted to regulate and control the practice by law so that only true murderers would be executed (Exod. 21:12-14). The cities of refuge were part of this continuing legal control of killings for vengeance (Deut. 19:1-10). As long as the old desert customs maintained their force, the avenger could not be replaced as executioner by a representative of the court. But he could be regularized. The entire law here protecting the innocent and calling for the death of the guilty shows how Israel in faith wrestled with the problem of violent killing. Because of her faith the life of every man was more precious in Israel than in any of the surrounding cultures, and she sought in this and other ways to prohibit killing.

The Daughters of Zelophehad (Num. 36:1-13)

This chapter is a sequel to 27:1-11, where the daughters of Zelophehad were granted the right to receive the inheritance of their sonless father. Their case now becomes the basis for a second promulgation of law on the inheritance rights of daughters. The heads of the Gileadite clan, to which they belonged, came forward to protest that the ordinance aimed at giving rights to these five women could lead to the clan's loss of the property if they married outside the tribe. If they did this, their land would eventually go to the tribe into which they married, and the original division of the land would be violated, the inheritance of one tribe passing to another. The land was the gift of the Lord to the tribe, whose rights must be protected.

Moses, seeing the justice of the protest, commands the five daughters of Zelophehad to marry only within the tribe of Manasseh. As in chapter 27, this specific case becomes binding on all. The inheritance of one tribe was not to be transferred to another, because each tribe's share of the Promised Land was the visible reality which constituted its portion in the Lord's promise and blessing.